Fine Art Children's Photography

Techniques and Images in Black & White

Doris Carol Doyle and Ian Doyle

Amherst Media, inc. ■ Buffalo, NY

DEDICATION:
This book is dedicated to my family: to my husband Ian and my daughters Chelsea and Sara, and to my sisters Lou Ann, Jo, and Nancy. It is also dedicated to the memory of my parents, Louise and Tony Stefaniak.

Published by:
Amherst Media, Inc.
P.O. Box 586
Buffalo, N.Y. 14226
Fax: 716-874-4508

Publisher: Craig Alesse
Senior Editor/Project Manager: Michelle Perkins
Copy Editor: Matthew A. Kreib

ISBN: 0-58428-010-7
Library of Congress Card Catalog Number: 99-72172

Printed in the United States of America.
10 9 8 7 6 5 4 3 2 1

Table of Contents

When I was is college I was an Art major, studying ceramics and glass blowing. I worked my way through school selling my art in galleries. I always loved photography but knew I could not make a living at it. I took classes in photography because of my love of it. That is where I met my husband Ian, a journalism and English major, who also knew you can't make a living in photography. With two such minds, we graduated and immediately went into photography big time and opened a commercial black and white photo lab.

We have run our lab, White Coyote Photo, for twenty years. As things will happen, I had my babies and I photographed them and then other peoples' babies also. Before I had my own children I didn't think I had the sensitivity or patience to be a good children's portrait photographer. I had done commercial work and location work for public relations firms, but I never really loved it like I do taking pictures of kids.

"I never really loved it like I do taking pictures of kids."

Rather than providing a linear "text book" on photographing children, this volume explores a selection of over fifty images. Each portrait is discussed individually to show how it was created. Lighting diagrams and equipment lists are included for each image to give you the technical information you need to explore your own variations on these successful portraits. The images are grouped topically to explore special subjects (like kids and their pets) and settings (such as studio and location portraits).

The majority of images discussed can be created with minimal equipment (any format camera, tripod, flash and/or reflector). Some require additional studio lighting equipment, but none are extremely equipment intensive. Rather, a focus is placed on creating unique poses, evaluating composition, working with children and the art of portrait photography. As such, this book provides an excellent manual for professionals seeking to add new dimension to their portraits, as well as for serious amateurs looking to create dramatic, professional-looking images of children.

I had to include one of the very first photographs I ever took. My father loved cameras and his new one was a Polaroid. He let me take this family shot, saying only not to cut off their heads. As nervous as I was, I didn't cut off their heads! This was the humble beginning of my career in photography

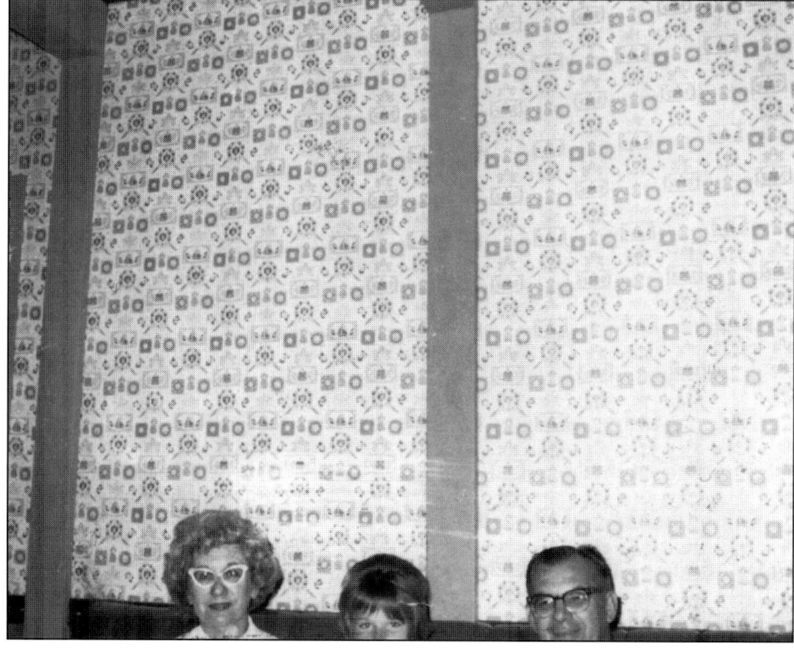

Studio Portraits

"When I work in our studio, I run around barefoot. I crawl around on the floor and chase infants. I also keep the studio warm and inviting, since comfort is my number one concern for my clients."

•Making Shoots Fun and Relaxed

Some of the best pictures happen when kids are just being themselves and having a good time. When I work in our studio, I run around barefoot. I have always found it easier and more comfortable. I crawl around on the floor, chase infants – and shoes just get in the way. I also keep the studio warm and inviting, since comfort is my number one concern for my clients. After all, relaxed people photograph the best.

"... the best pictures happen when kids are just being themselves ..."

•Talking with Kids

As I shoot, I talk to the kids about school, their best friends, sports they are interested in – whatever they want to talk about. When the kids start talking about themselves, they forget that there is someone sitting there with a camera pointed at them.

It's also helpful to have a repertoire of silly jokes. Parents tend to roll their eyes, but kids love them. We also have lots of hats hanging on the wall in the studio. There's even a box full of toys that can be fun to play with. It's never a mistake to have fun and play while working.

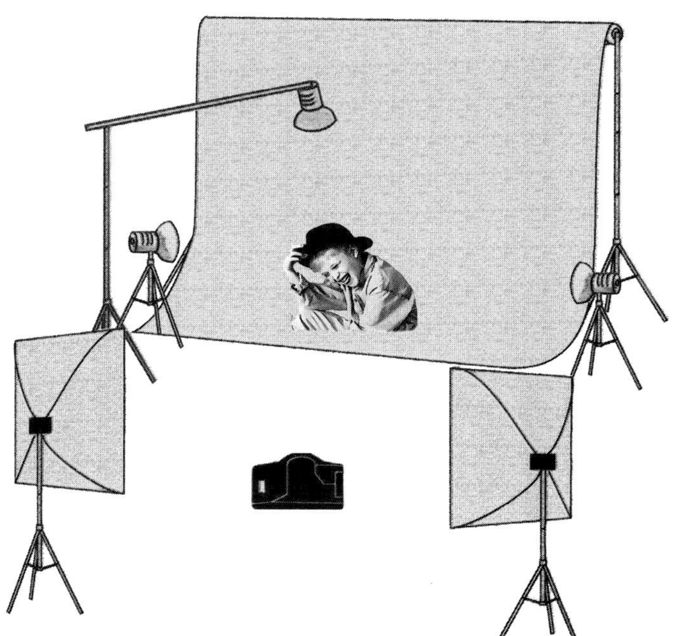

Camera: Canon EOS

Lens: 35-135mm

Film: Ilford XP1, rated at E.I. 200

The photograph was illuminated using five lights. Two softboxes were placed near the camera to either side of the subject. The softbox on the left provided the main light, while the soft box to the right was set at 1/2 power to provide fill light. Two additional lights were used to throw light onto the background. Finally, a hair light was positioned above the subject on a boom.

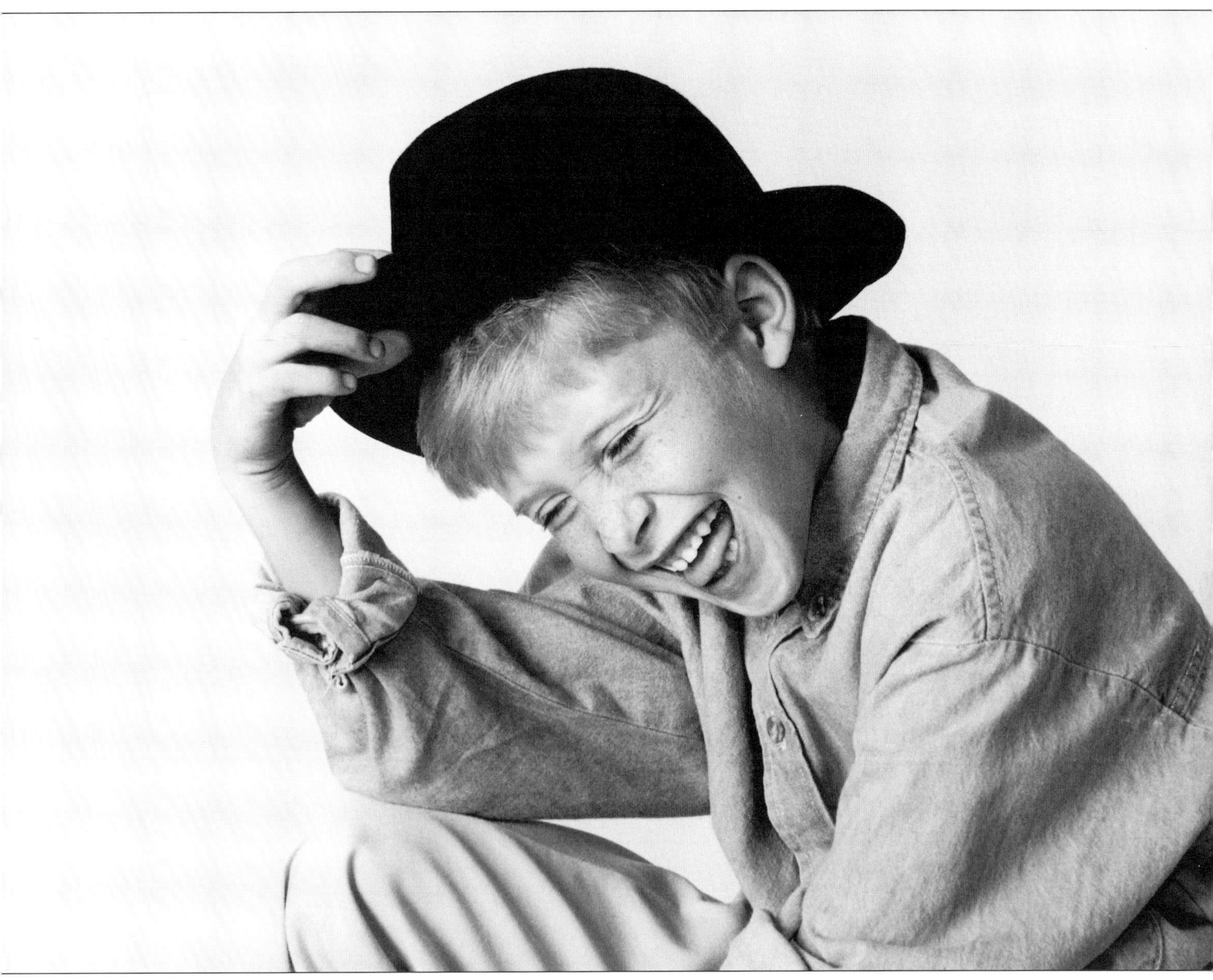

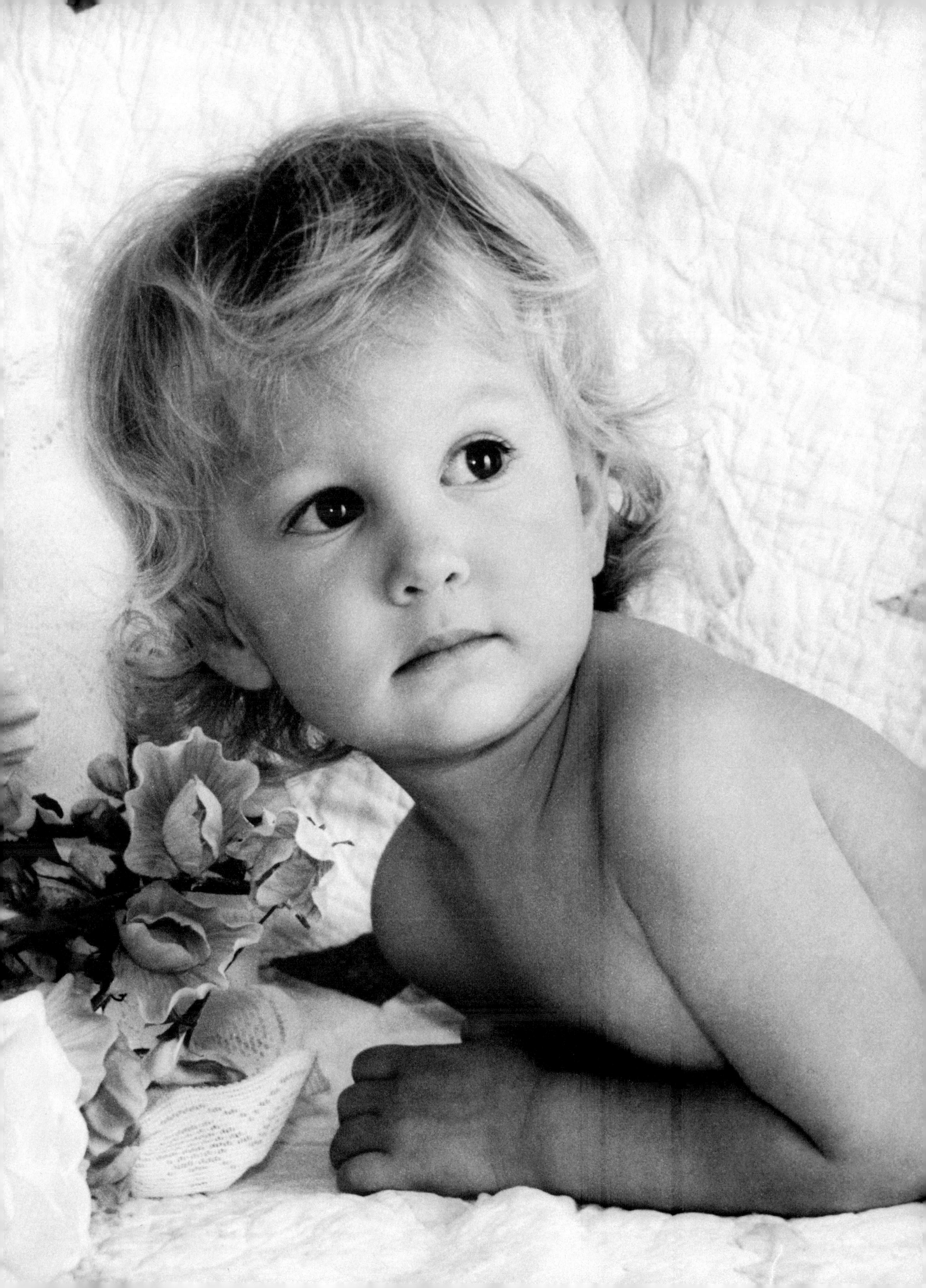

"I photographed practically everyone on the block ..."

•Shooting at Home

I think that most everyone starts in their kitchen or their living room when they begin taking pictures for other people. You shove away the furniture and setup the props and the background and you have an instant studio. This is one of the earlier photo sessions that we did. In fact, this photo was taken in our kitchen.

We threw an antique quilt over a bench seat and moved it up against a wall. We asked the little girl to lay on her stomach, because the quilt wasn't as big as a studio backdrop. The space was limited, so we moved in for a head-and-shoulders shot.

When I was getting started, I photographed practically everyone on the block, and all the neighbor kids. I did it for next to nothing in order to build a portfolio and learn. Everyone has to start somewhere!

•Lighting

This picture was lit with a 500 watt tungsten light behind a diffusion panel on the right side of the frame, and diffused window light on the left. An on-camera flash unit provided fill light.

Camera: Canon FTB manual camera

Lens: 50mm

Film: Ilford XP1 rated at E.I. 200

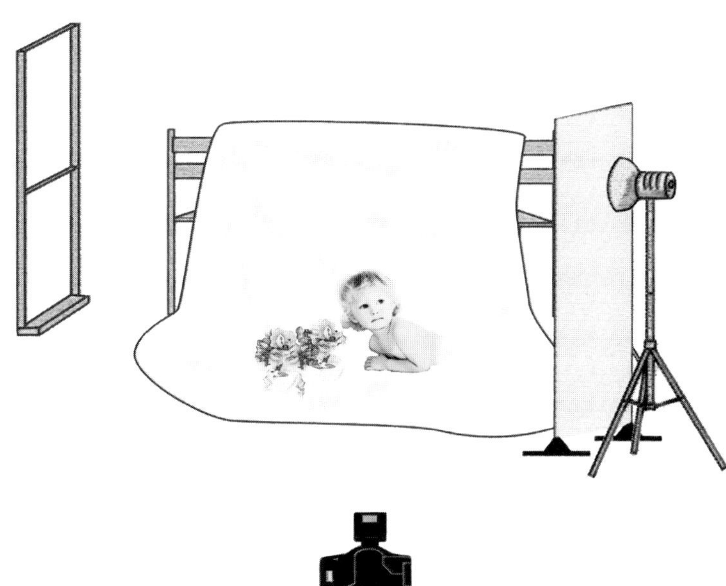

Three light sources were used to capture this image. Window light hits the subject from the left, and a 500 watt tungsten light shines through a diffusion screen to the right. Fill light was provided by an on-camera flash.

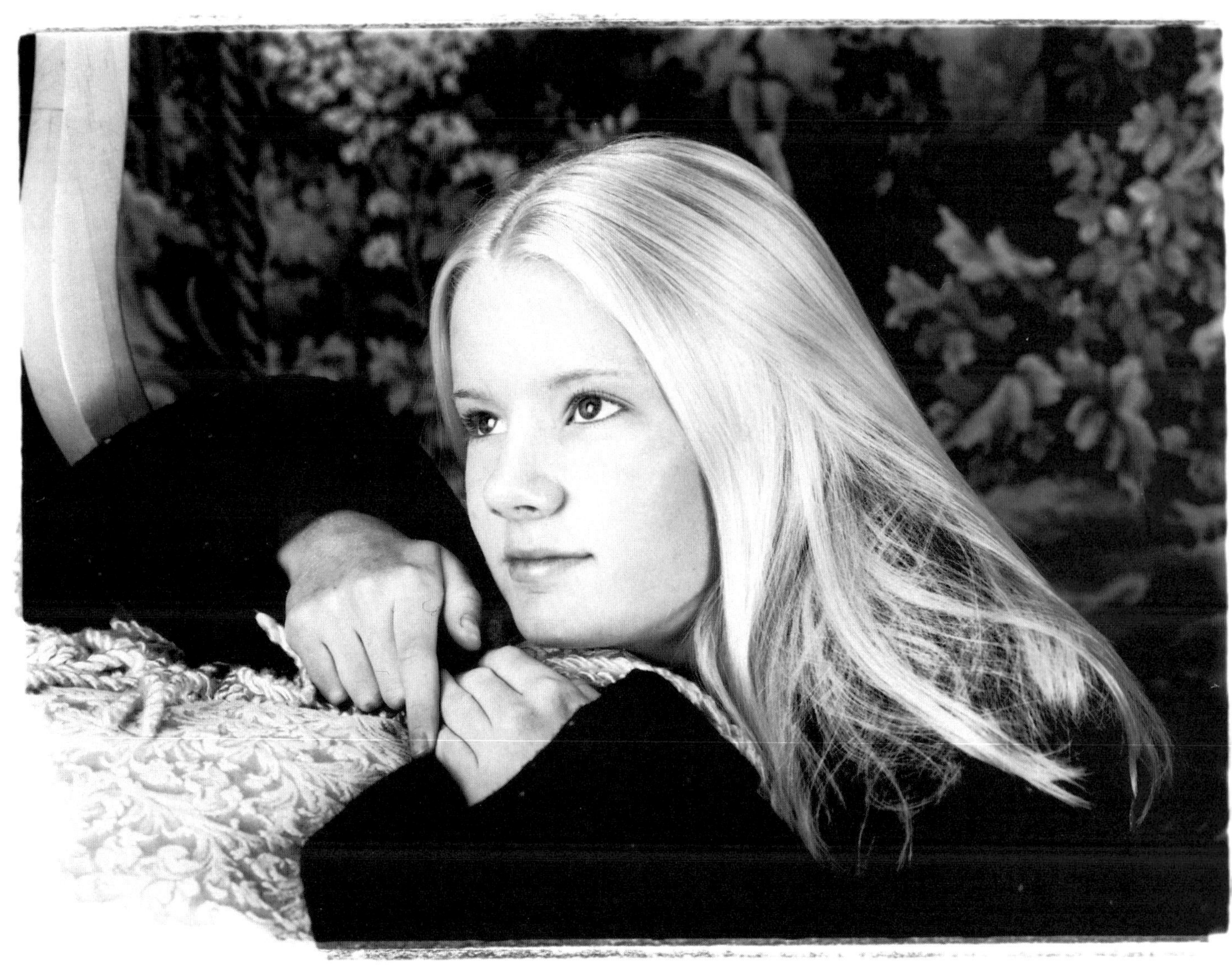

"... seat the subject a little lower than the camera ..."

•Window to the Soul

You know the old saying that the eyes are the window to the soul. For exactly this reason, in portraiture the first thing that you gravitate to is the eyes.

One way to emphasize the importance of the eyes is to seat subjects a little lower than the camera and have them look up into the light. This shows more of the whites of their eyes and makes the eyes look bigger, and brighter and very flattering.

•Lens Selection

We shot this image with the Pentax 645 and a 200mm lens. The longer focal length lens gives us a narrower depth of field than a normal focal length lens so that the background appears soft and out of focus. This tends to add greater depth to the photo because the sharp focus of the subject stands her apart from the softer background.

•Border Effect

When printing, we used the full frame of the negative. Filing out the negative carrier allowed the whole negative and some of the sprocket holes to show. This technique creates a different style of image for our clients to choose from.

Camera: Pentax 645

Lens: 200mm

Film: Kodak TMX 100

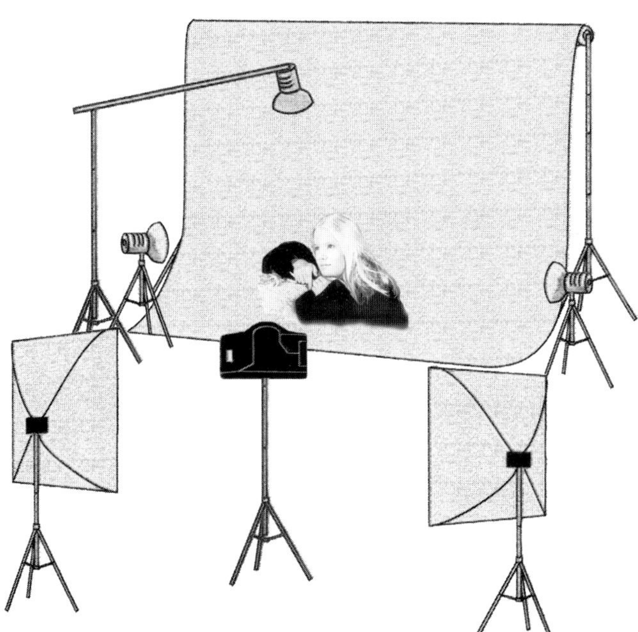

The photograph was illuminated using five lights. Two softboxes were placed near the camera to either side of the subject. The softbox on the left provided the main light, while the soft box to the right was set at 1/2 power to provide fill light. Two additional lights were used to throw light onto the background. Finally, a hair light was positioned above the subject on a boom.

•Simplicity

The beauty of this picture is its simplicity. The little girl is looking straight into the camera which gives you a direct connection with her. For a final touch, we placed flowers in the foreground which mimicked the flowers on her hat.

"... play dress-up and you'll make their day."

•High Key Lighting

We shoot a high key portrait by creating a shadowless white background which is exposed one to one and a half stops brighter than the subject.

•Make Her Day

Ask little girls if they would like to play dress-up and you'll make their day. This is the daughter of a good friend who owns a wonderful children's clothing store, so we had our choice of outfits. Sometimes translucent powder on a make-up brush transforms the ordinary into fantasy. Hats, flowers, bracelets, or necklaces can especially help little girls get into their make-believe world. For boys, it's sports, hats and toys. We have trains, cars – a whole box of toys. I always have my eyes open for cute hats for boys, since these are harder to find than girls' hats.

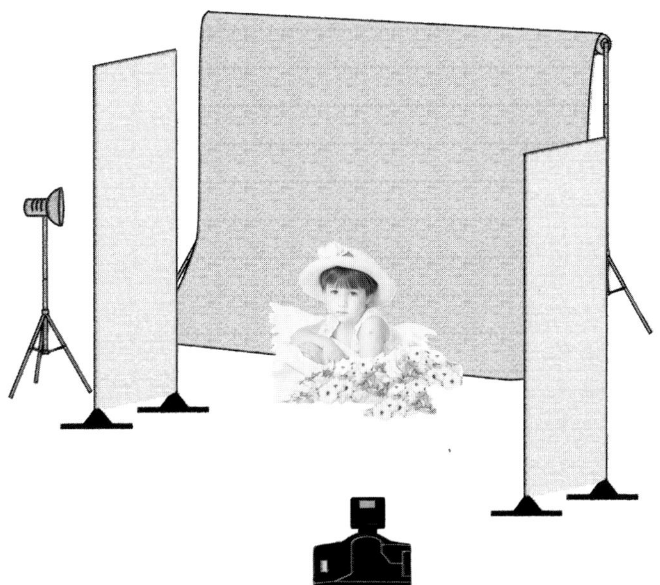

Camera: Canon FTB

Lens: 50mm, f-1.8

Film: Ilford XP1, rated at E.I. 200

The secret to successful high key lighting portraiture is using enough light to keep the background and subject well illuminated. Here, a tungsten light hits the background and subject through a diffusion panel, and a reflector panel bounces some of this light back from the other side of the set. An on-camera flash completes the set-up.

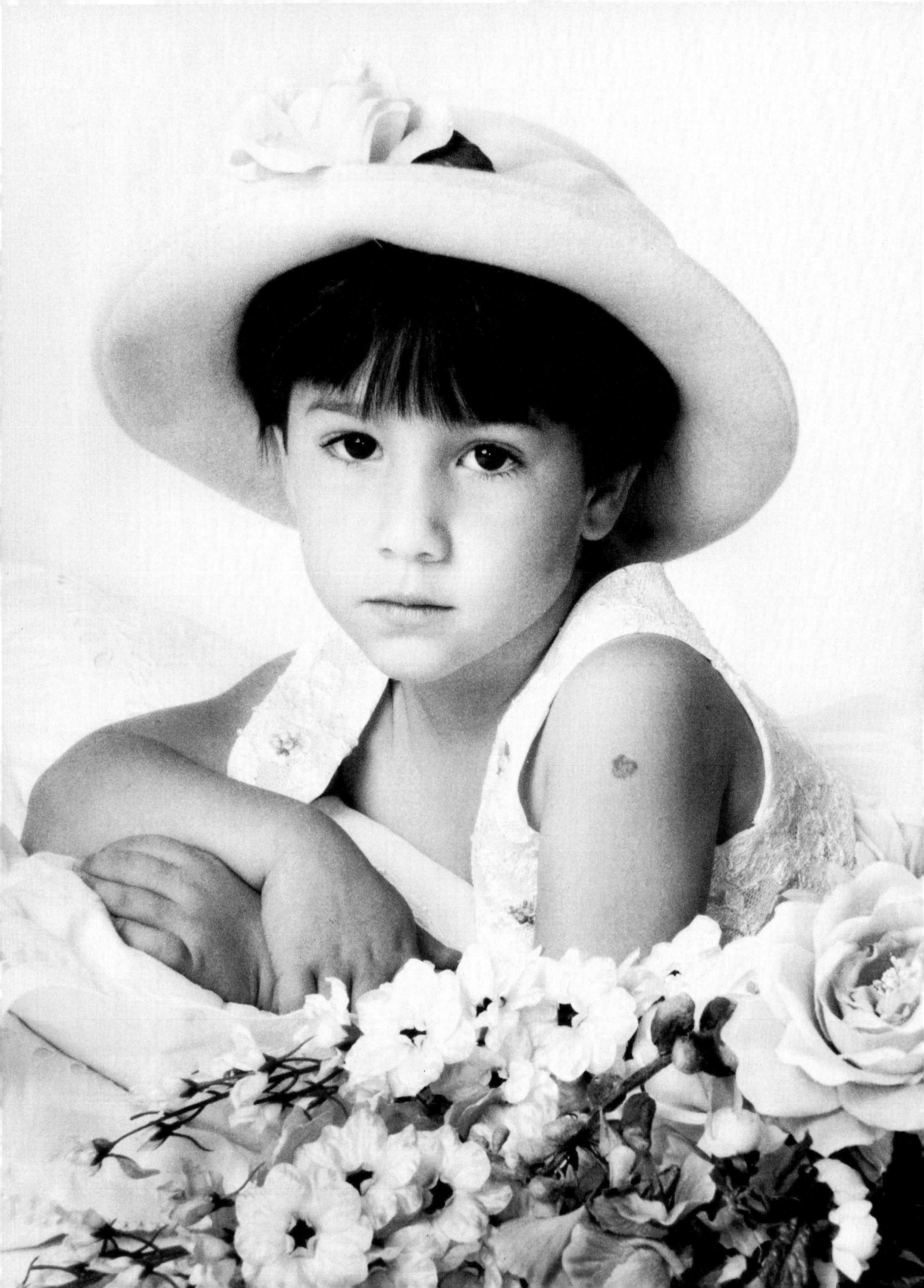

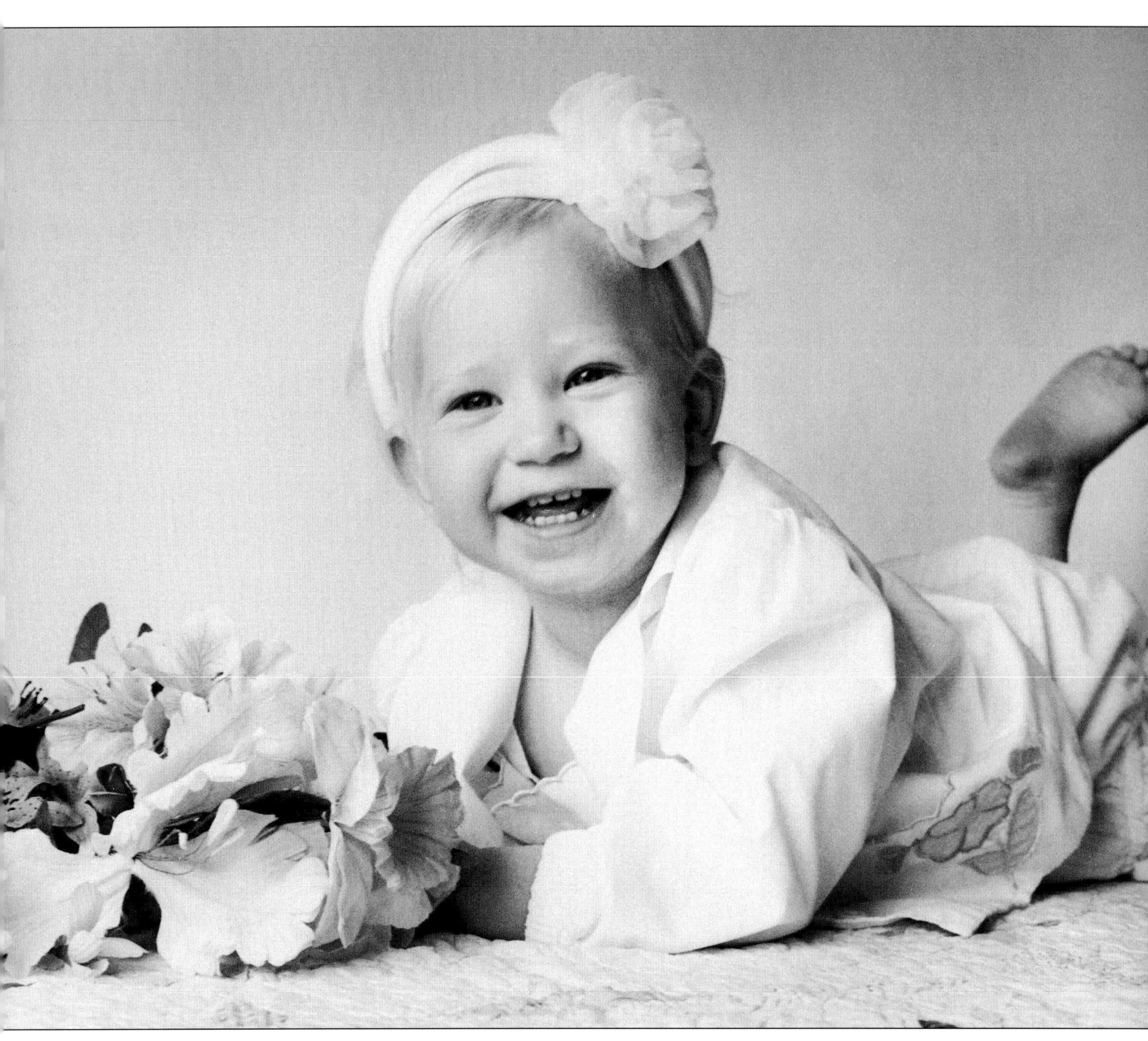

"They are ready to fly at all times ..."

•Limited Attention Spans

It is always challenging and fun to engage a one and a half year old for any length of time. Needless to say, their attention span is not that long. They are ready to fly at all times and our job is keep them distracted long enough to get a sweet picture.

•Using Props

We like to use antique baby quilts in the studio. It makes a nice soft surface for the children to lay on and it also makes a very pretty prop. We used to buy fresh flowers for shoots but we really don't want them eaten or bitten by little ones. Silk flowers are almost indestructible and they add a nice grounding effect to a composition. We also have a zoo of stuffed animals, and even soap bubbles (you never know when someone might be in the mood!).

Props are wonderful, but don't fall into the trap of shooting props at the expense of a good portrait. A beautiful set-up can make a subject look good, but what we try to do is capture what's unique about each child. That said, when we use props they are not the important element in the photo. Rather, they set a scene in which the child can feel comfortable.

Camera: Canon FTB

Lens: 50mm Canon f-1.8

Film: Kodak Plus X

As in the previous image, here a tungsten light hits the background and subject through a diffusion panel, and a reflector panel bounces some of this light back from the other side of the set. An on-camera flash completes the set-up.

•Capturing Special Moments

One of the wonderful things that we get to do as photographers is capture small moments of time and record them – moments that happen now and perhaps will never be repeated again. Some days, it's a pretty neat job.

"Some days, it's a pretty neat job."

In this particular instance, the main reason why the Mom brought her daughter into the studio for a portrait session was to document her beautiful hair. The girl had decided that it was time to have shorter hair. After the photos were taken, mom and daughter went to the hair salon and she had it all cut off.

•Lighting

This photo is shot with two lights. There is a big soft box off to the right, a hair light from above, and a large reflector panel to the right of the camera position. By having the girl look away from the main light and into the reflector you keep the soft shading on the face. This is a good example of broad lighting where the soft box is illuminating the side of the face that is facing the camera.

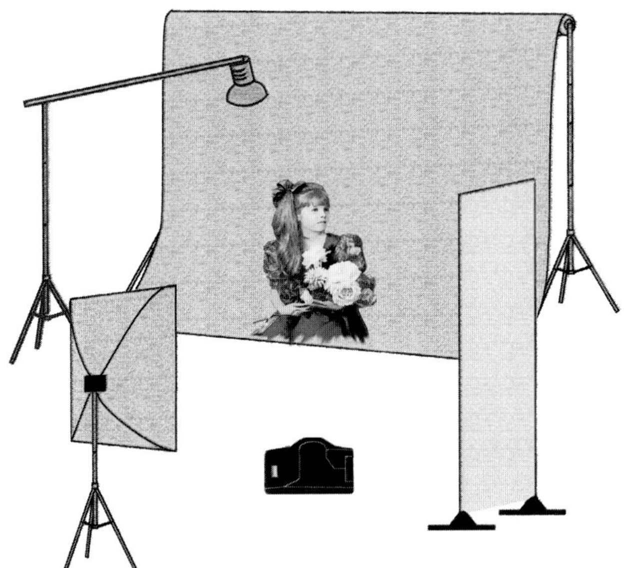

Camera: Canon EOS

Lens: 50mm Canon f-1.8

Film: Kodak Plus-X, rated at E.I. 125

This image was shot using a big soft box off to the right, a hair light from above, and a large reflector panel to the right of the camera position. It is a good example of a set-up for broad lighting.

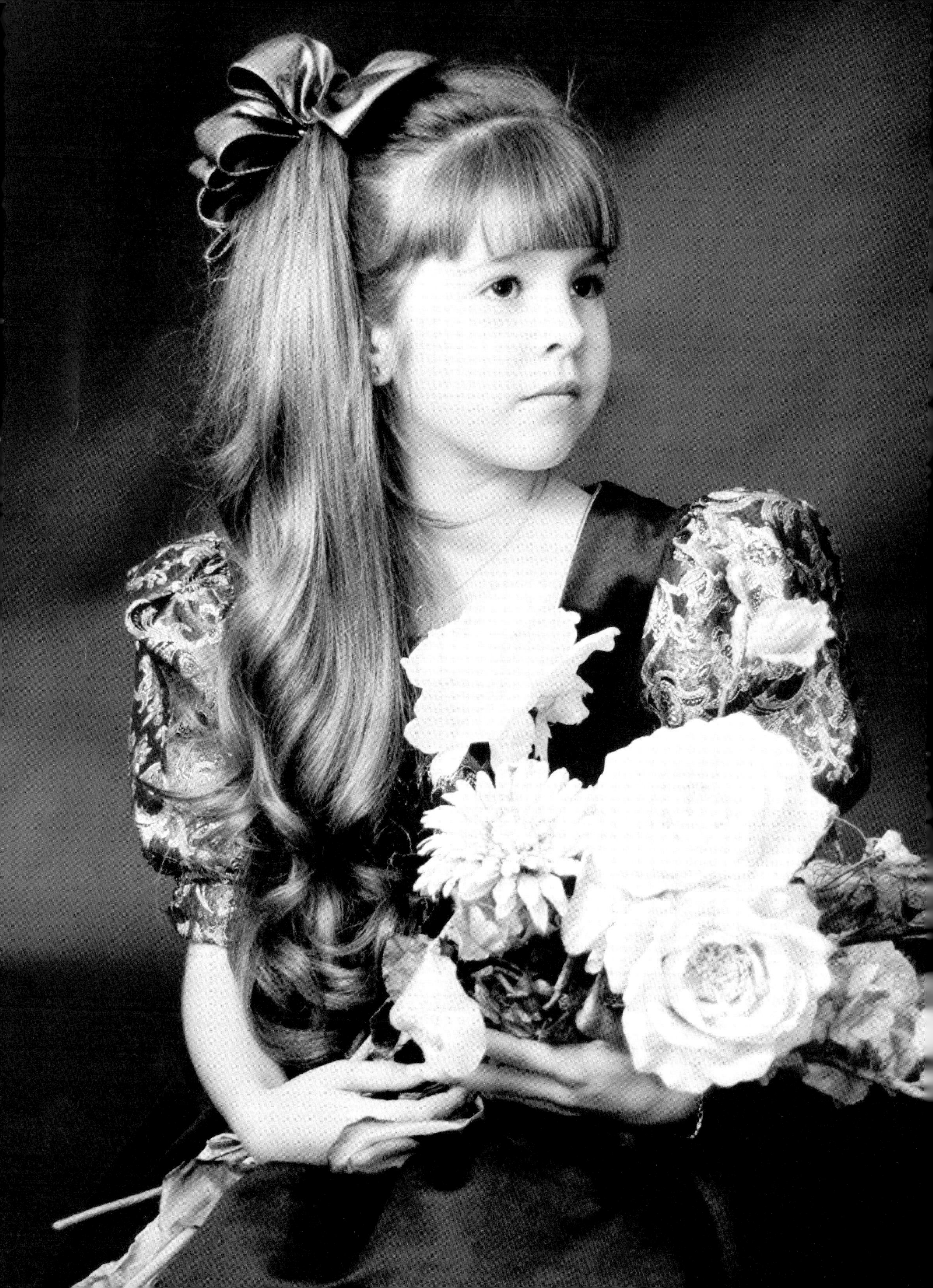

•Hands Reveal Comfort

I always like to look at people's hands when I look at photographs. You can see stress and tension in their hands more often than you can see it in their faces. If their hands seem relaxed, you know the subject is really at ease.

This little fellow looks very comfortable with the setting and very composed. His stance is loose and unrestrained – something you can tell by looking at his relaxed little hands. His left hand is hanging leisurely by his side and his other hand is clasping (very gingerly) a leaf on the plant.

"His stance is loose and unrestrained ..."

•Clothing

This young boy is about eighteen months old, but his clothing belies his age. He looks very grown up because he is dressed is this very sophisticated tuxedo.

•Setting

Peach colored sheer fabric on the floor gives this photograph an ethereal look. The setting is simple with a minimum of props to distract us from the subject.

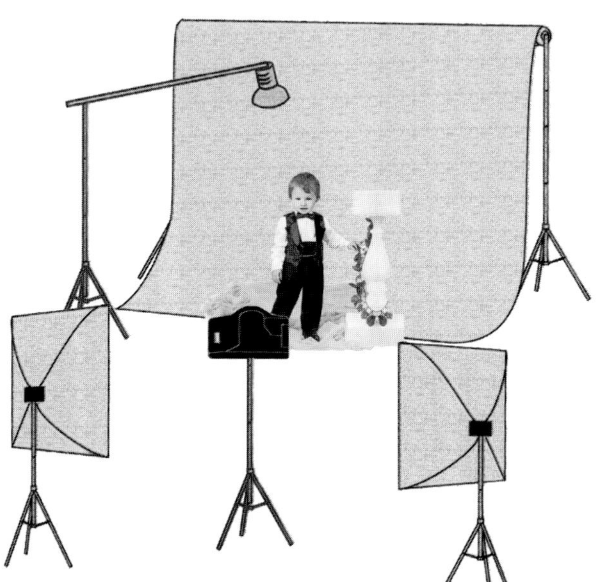

Camera: Pentax 645
Lens: 75mm leaf-shutter
Film: Kodak TMX 100

The main light for this shot comes from a softbox placed to the left of the camera. Another softbox is used at half-power from the right side of the camera to provide fill light. A hair light was added above the subject on a boom.

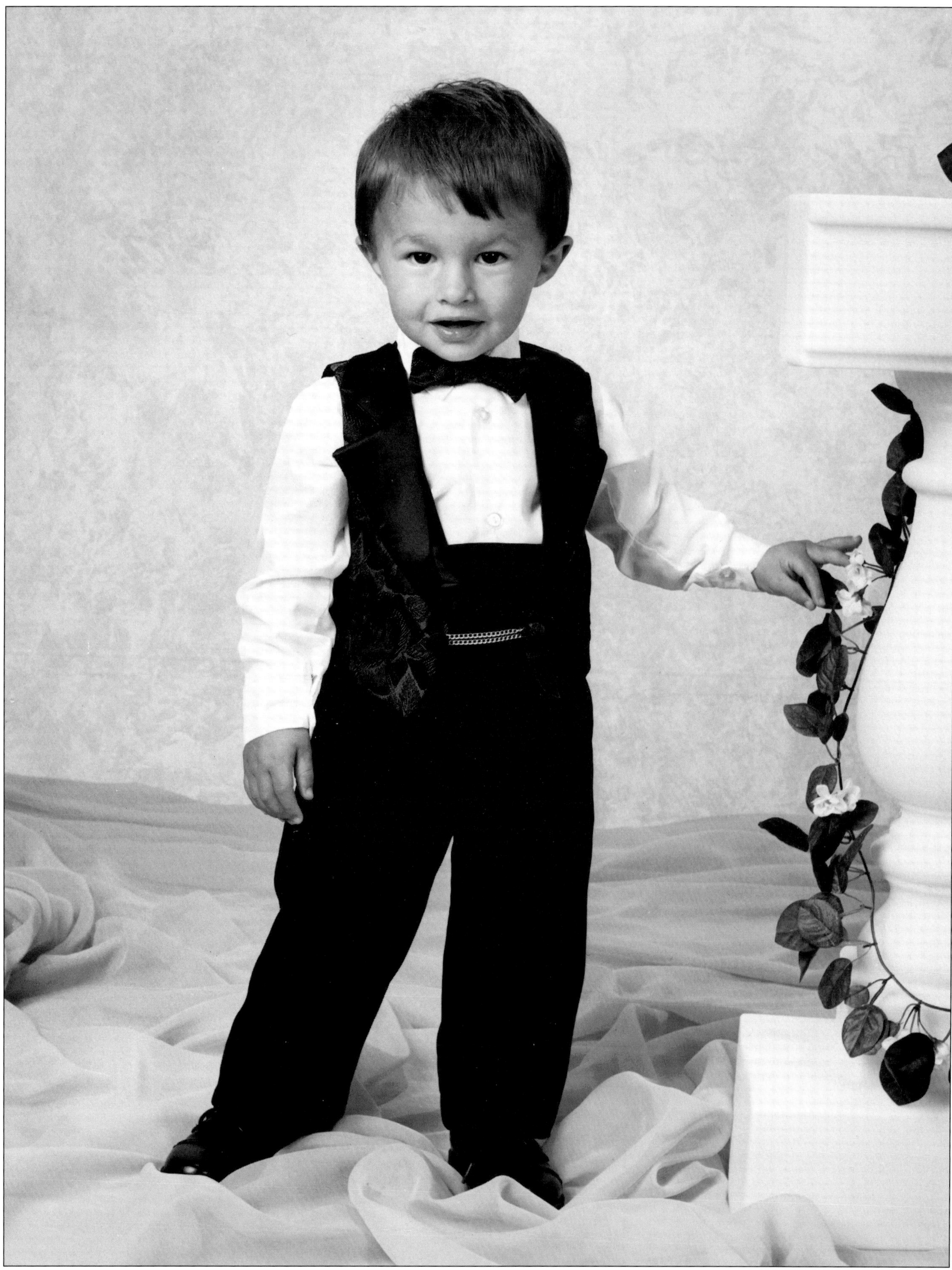

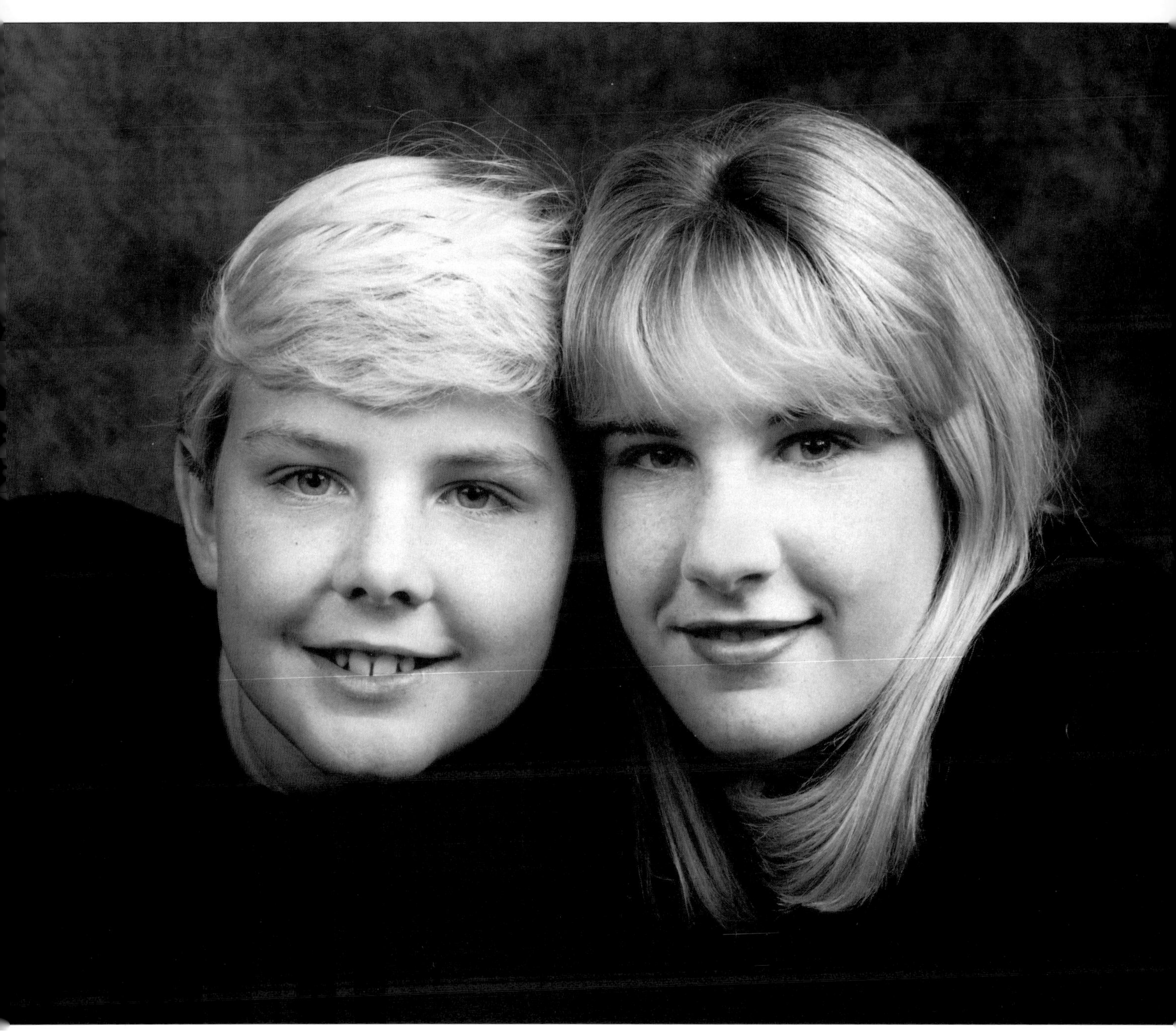

•Butterfly Lighting

The lighting for this portrait is "butterfly lighting," so called because it makes a "butterfly" shadow under the nose. It is also characterized by full lighting on the face. This helps define the facial features and sculpt the face. It presents a natural-looking portrait because it mimics the way the sun lights people's faces – one light shining from above. This type of lighting is simply done by having one light source elevated directly above the camera lens.

"You can see the family resemblance ..."

•Composition

The dark background and the dark clothing offset the light skin tone and hair of the subjects. Both subjects are looking directly into the camera so that it appears that they are looking directly at you. You can see the family resemblance, particularly since they have their heads so close that they are touching.

•Low Key

The low key approach used here is more appropriate for older kids, giving a more serious look to the portrait. With smaller children or babies, a lighter, more airy look is sometimes more appealing.

Camera: Pentax 645

Lens: 75mm leaf-shutter

Film: Kodak TMX 100 rated at E.I. 80

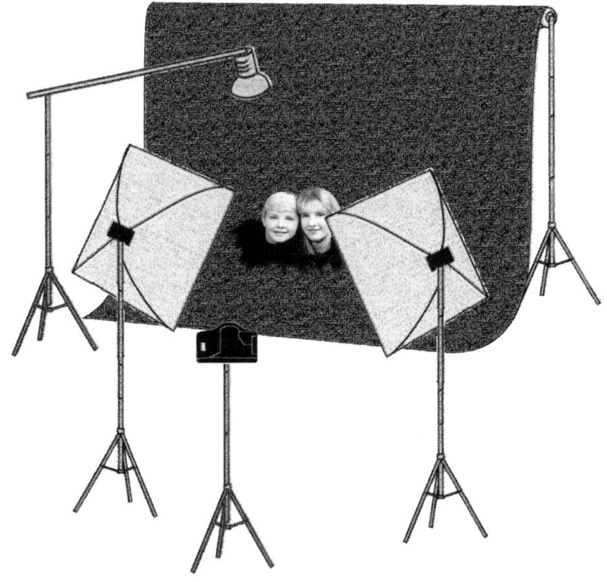

Two soft boxes are placed immediately to the left and right of the camera. They are raised high and cast light down on the subjects. A hair light was then added on a boom above the subjects.

•Two and Three Year Olds

When kids are two or three years old, most of the time they are on full throttle. You can expend a lot of energy just trying to keep them still. At times you have to play games and sing songs to keep their attention focused.

•Flying Teddy Bears

In our studio we have teddy bears. We have one special little bear named Timmy, Timmy's brother and his close relative, Timmy's cousin. Their specialty is flying. An assistant will be performing teddy bear acrobatics directly behind the camera. All these antics help to catch exceptional looks like this one.

"Their specialty is flying."

•Putting Kids at Ease

An integral part of the job of being a photographer is to be entertaining and engaging with these youngsters. They are in a foreign environment and they can easily get timid in front of the camera. Most adults don't like to have their picture taken. They are intimidated by cameras, and it's no different for kids.

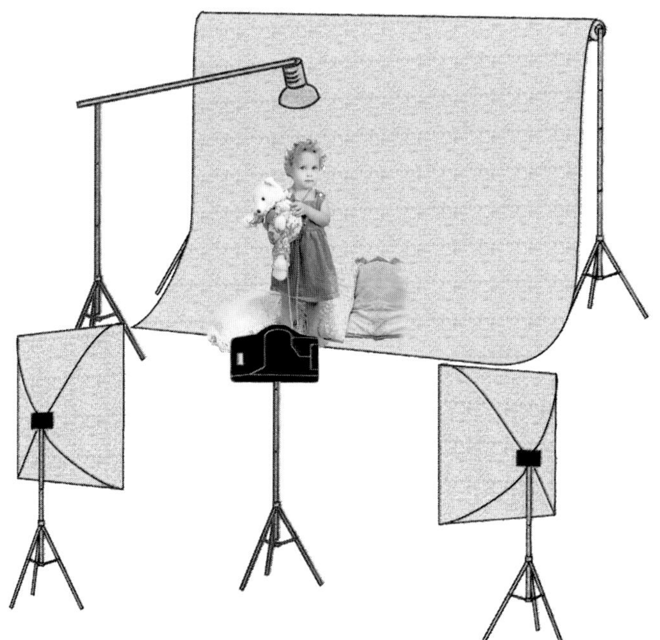

Camera: Pentax 645
Lens: 75mm leaf-shutter
Film: Kodak TMX 100
Exposure: f-9.5 at 1/90 sec.

The main light for this shot comes from a softbox placed to the left of the camera. Another softbox is used at half-power from the right side of the camera to provide fill light. A hair light was added above the subject on a boom.

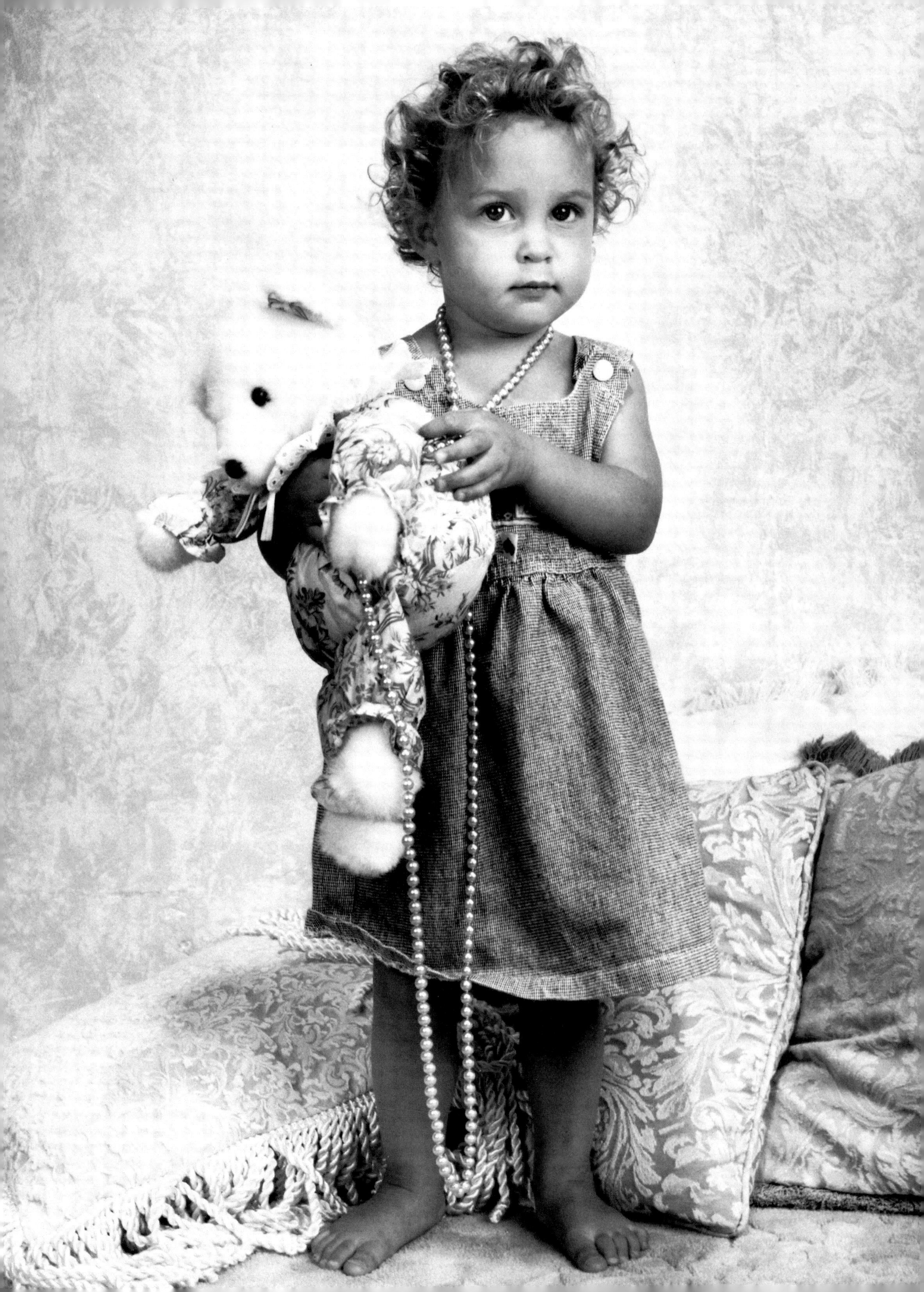

•Treat them with Dignity

Teenagers are often dragged into the studio with their family for portraits. They would rather be anywhere else. We find that if you treat them with some dignity and give them some choices about how they would like to be photographed, they usually respond positively. We say "usually" because it doesn't *always* work out that way. There is no getting around that fact that teenagers will be teenagers.

"They would rather be anywhere else."

We always ask teenagers if they have seen a portrait that they liked. We also offer them the option of bringing a change of clothes – a favorite dress or shirt can make them feel comfortable and relaxed. We also see what settings they prefer and show them other portraits we've taken of teenagers. Spending a little extra time with teenagers allows them a little more control.

•Lighting

In this shot we used a strobe light with only a reflector. We used no soft box or diffusion on the light at all. We wanted the quality of the light to be a little more directional. This allowed us to keep the side of his face away from the light fairly dark, and we feathered the light (or turned it) so that it wouldn't spill over on to the backdrop because we wanted it to stay dark. This kind of pose makes it easier for a teenage subject to look good and yet not feel "posed."

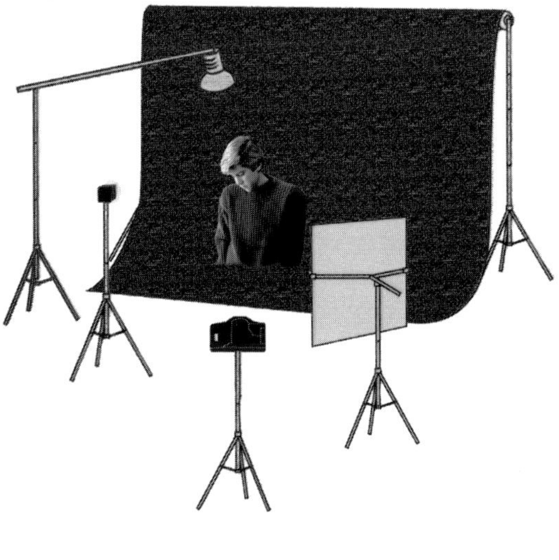

Camera: Canon EOS

Lens: 50mm Canon f-1.8

Film: Kodak Plus-X, rated at E.I. 125

The main light for this shot comes from a bare strobe light placed to the left of the camera. A hair light was added above the subject on a boom. A reflector panel was added to the right of the camera close to the subject to kick back fill light.

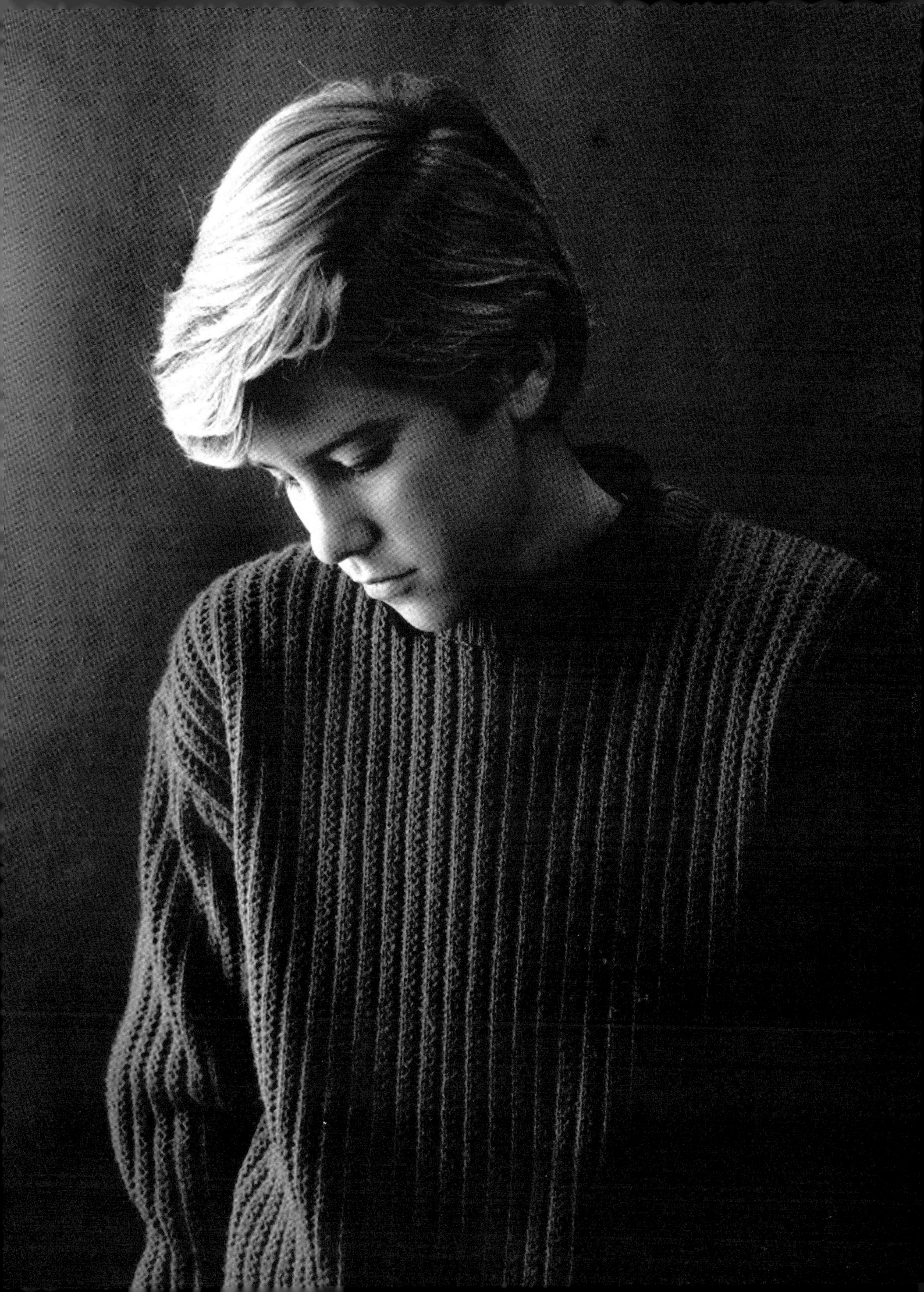

•Capturing Personality

This picture captures this little girl's unique personality. It is a simple and sweet childlike moment.

"... a simple and sweet childlike moment."

•Lighting

This was one of the earlier photo session that we did. It was taken with an on-camera flash which, when fired, triggered another strobe with a slave. That strobe was placed behind a translucent fabric diffusion screen.This strobe light was feathered so that it shone onto the background, making the white seamless background appear shadowless.

We used this kind of lighting scheme a while ago, particularly when we knew we were going to be hand coloring the photograph. It makes for a very low contrast image and it is perfect for hand coloring. This system worked well for starting the business, but eventually we found the on-camera flash to be limited. The light was too frontal and created some undesirable shadows. As we learned more about lighting, the shortcomings of this system became obvious.

Currently, we prefer a more flexible set-up. Using large softboxes with Norman flash heads allows for more controllable light. Our current 800 watt/second system is quite portable but provides plenty of light for my style of portraiture.

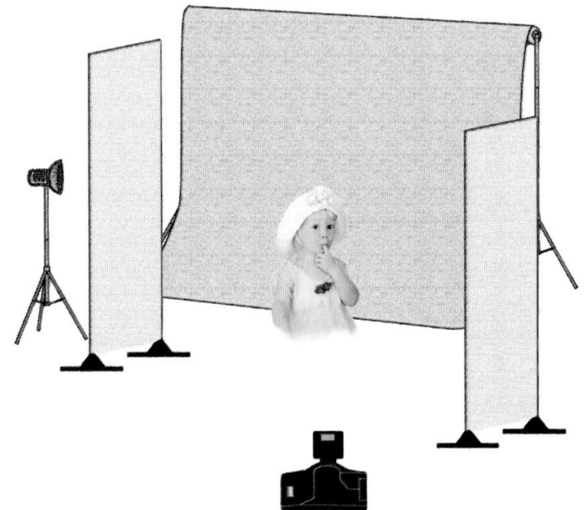

Camera: Canon EOS 630

Lens: 50mm

Film: Ilford XP1, rated at E.I. 200

As in the previous image, here a tungsten light hits the background and subject through a diffusion panel, and a reflector panel bounces some of this light back from the other side of the set. An on-camera flash completes the set-up.

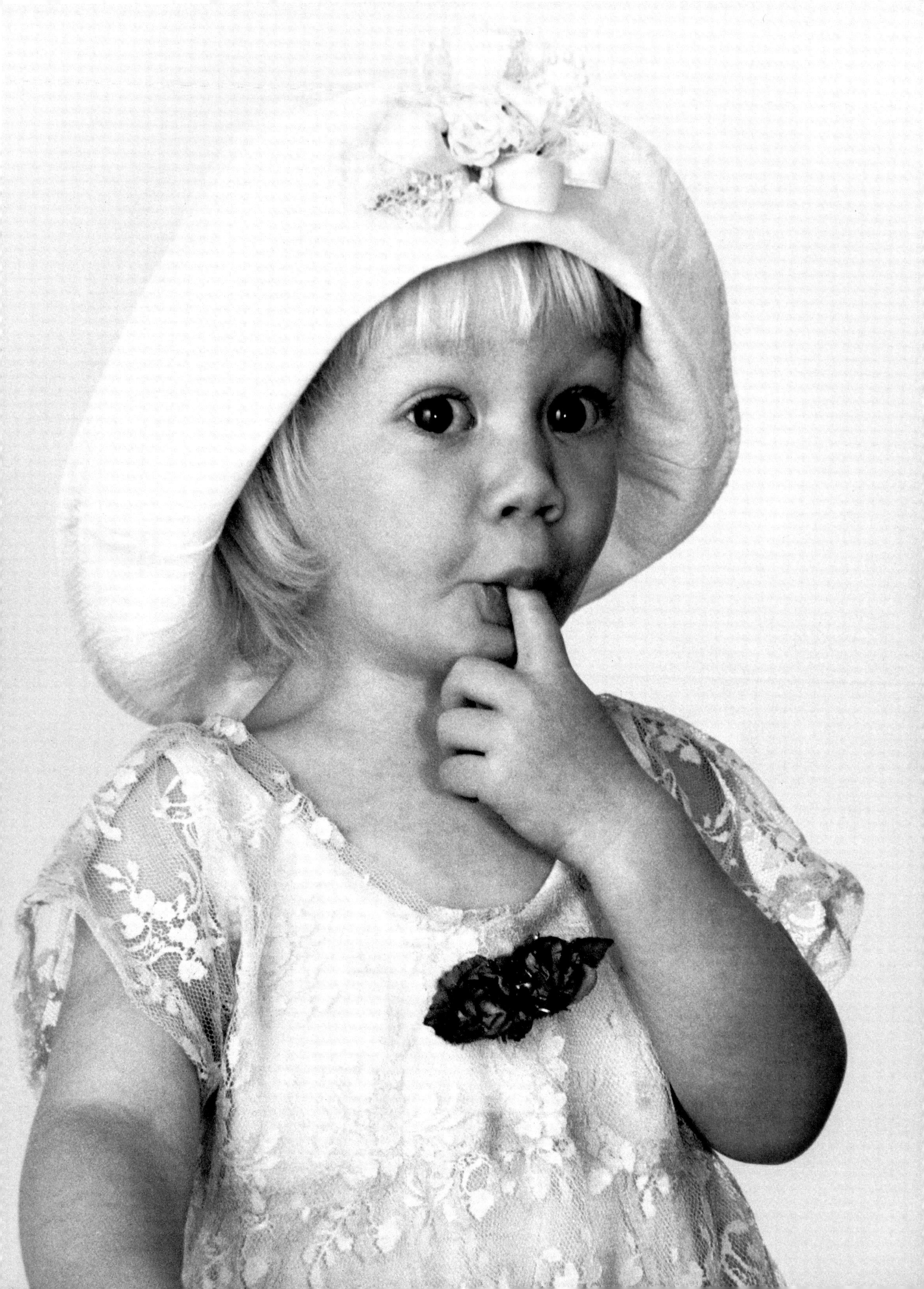

•Tickling

One of the best aspects of doing a lot of children's photography is you never really know what's going to happen. You always have to be ready for the unexpected. This splendid photo occurred by just suggesting to the little girl that she give her little brother a tickle. We got a wonderful response!

"You always have to be ready for the unexpected."

•Shoes

During the consultation when people book a session, we always talk about clothing. We make the usual suggestions about solid color clothing and the like and I usually tell parents (or grandparents, as in this case) not to bother with shoes. Little feet are better than any kind of shoe we can possibly put on them.

When we asked this little girl to take off her shoes she really didn't want to. We found that it was much better to acquiesce to her wishes than try to force her to do something she didn't want to do. If you respect the children's wishes and show them that you respect their needs, it makes everything run more smoothly.

•Using Timidity to Your Advantage

Younger children usually have only about twenty minutes of shooting in them. They may be a little shy until they begin to feel comfortable, and this is the best time to start shooting. Once they get used to us and lose that timidity, we have to start working on distractions to get their cooperation.

Camera: Pentax 645
Lens: 75mm leaf shutter
Film: Kodak TMAX100

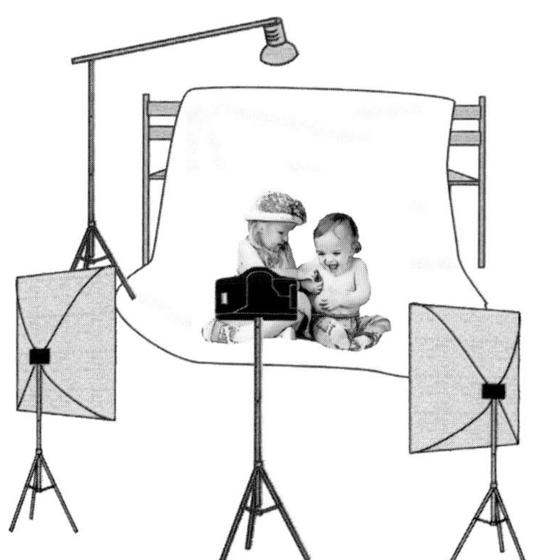

The main light for this shot comes from a softbox placed to the left of the camera. Another softbox is used at half-power from the right side of the camera to provide fill light. A hair light was added above the subject on a boom.

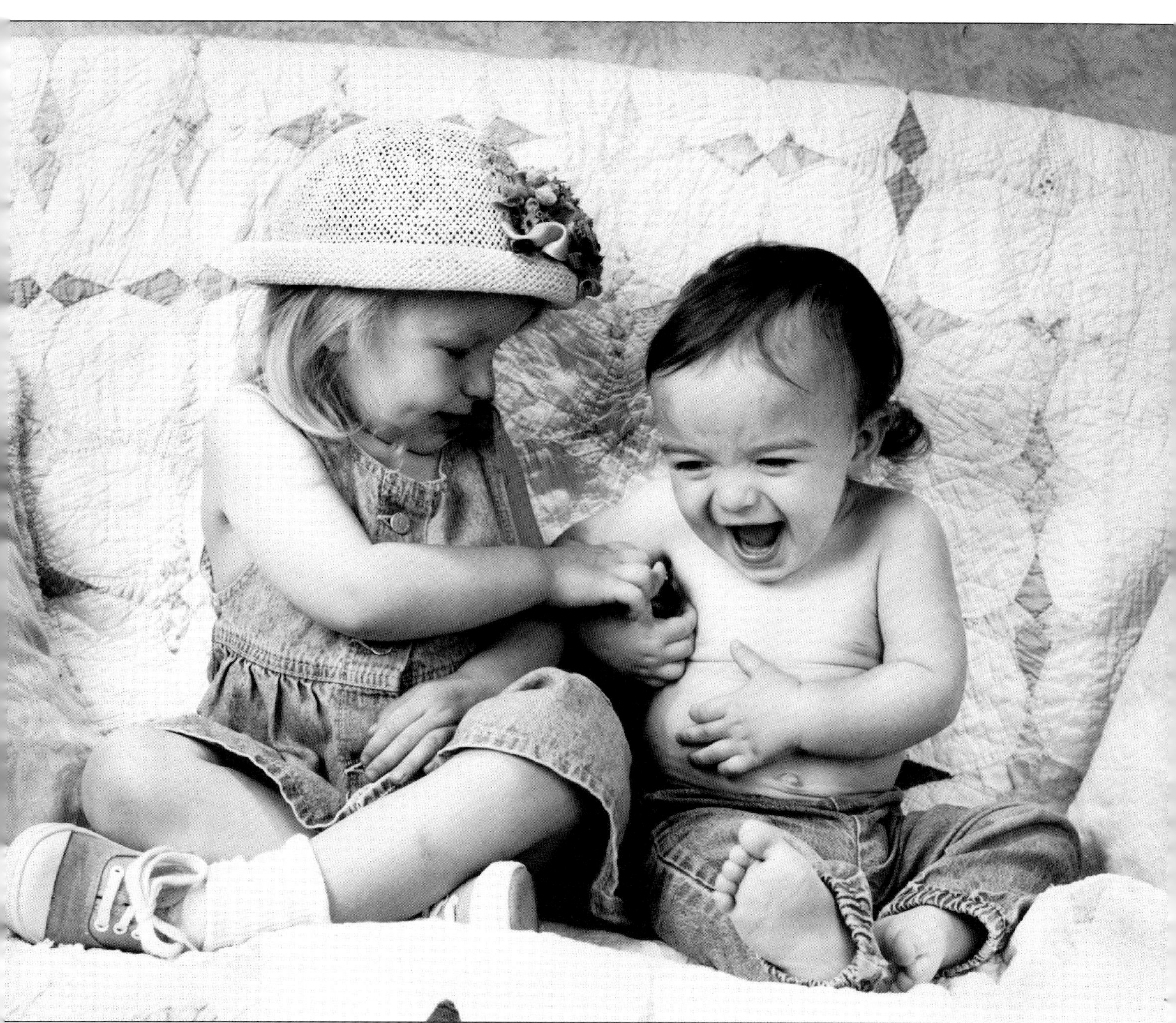

•Posing on the Floor

We spend a lot of time crawling around on the floor. Since most of our portraiture is informal we like to have a nest of pillows and carpeting as a set in which to shoot.

"We spend a lot of time crawling around on the floor."

•Clothing Selection

These girls are all dressed the same in overalls and long sleeved white shirts. We prefer to have long sleeved shirts or sleeveless shirts because we think it looks better to have a solid look to the arms and not have the "break" in tone midway down the arm that you get with a short sleeved shirt.

•Composition

They are arranged in a diamond pattern so that your eye travels around the diamond of faces and tends to pause on the face of each girl.

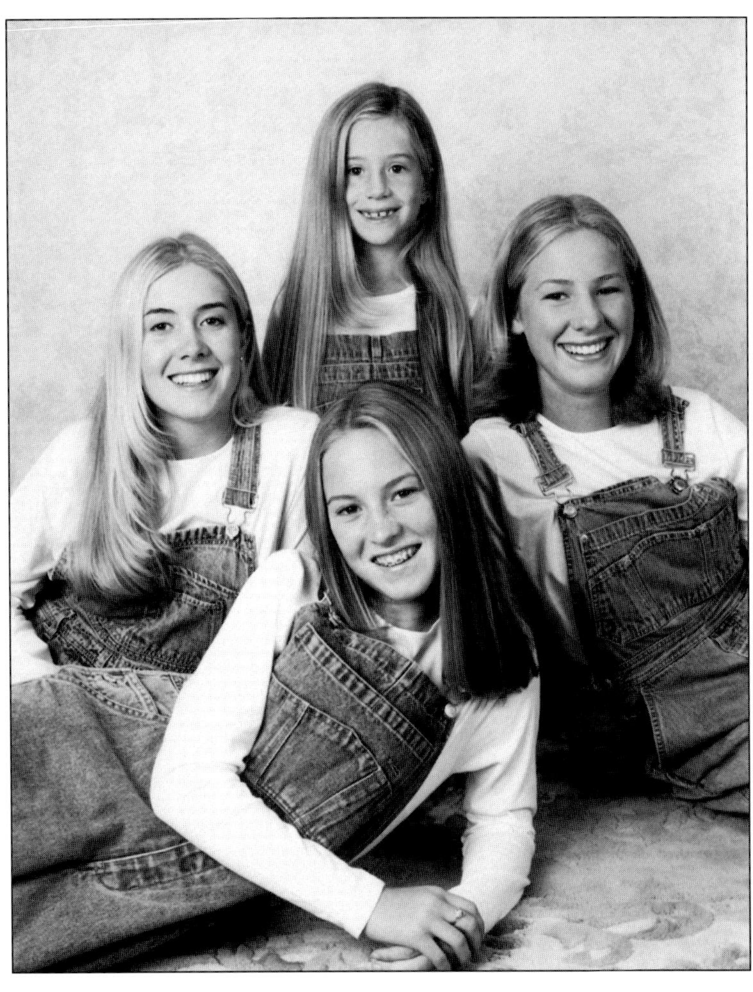

Camera: Pentax 645 on tripod
Lens: 75mm leaf shutter
Film: Kodak TMX 100, rated at E.I. 80

INFANTS

"It's a privilege to be able to photograph the new members of a family as it grows. We establish a good relationship with our clients so that they regularly bring back their children to us to have them photographed."

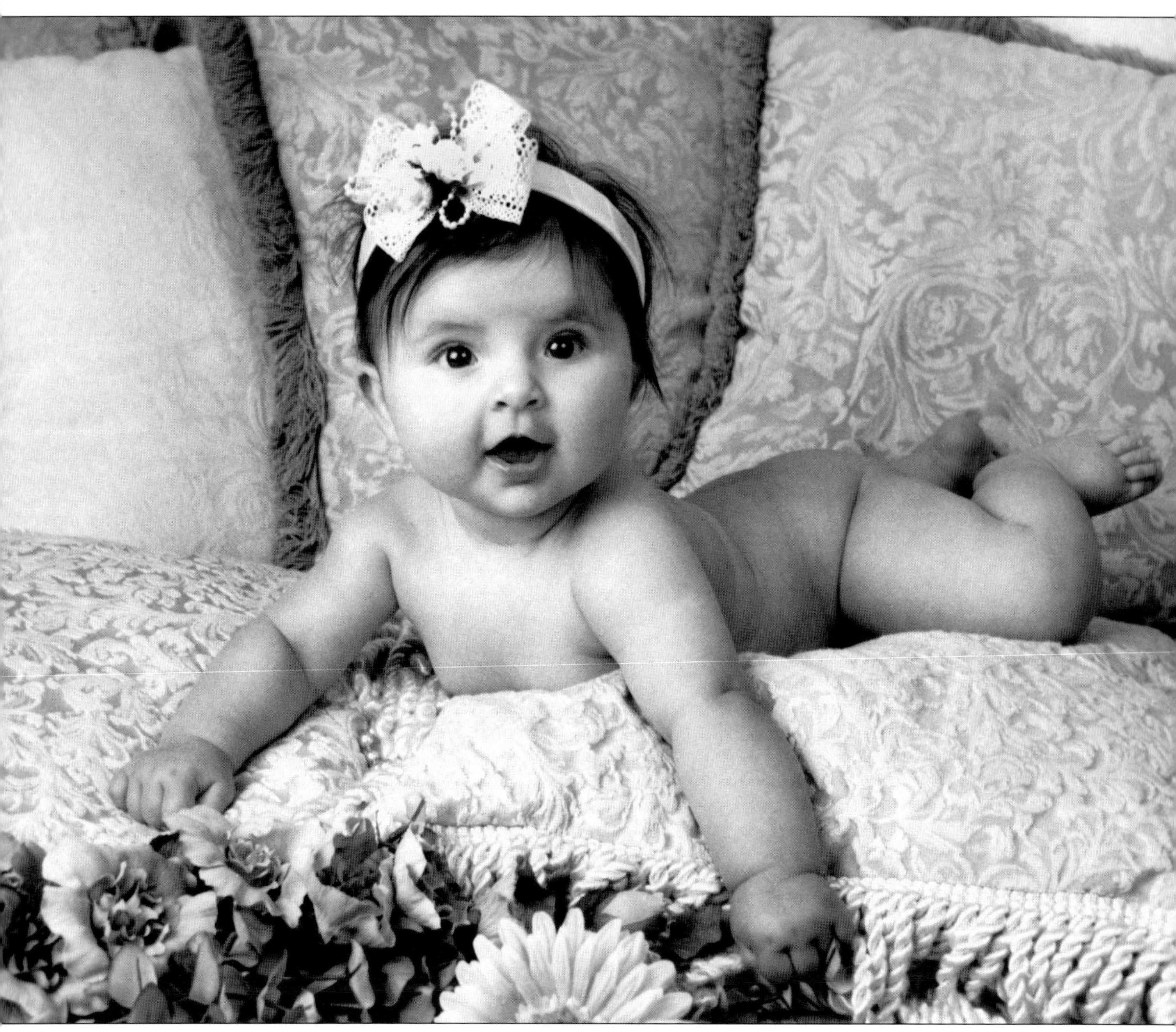

"Naked baby shots are classic ..."

•A Classic Shot

Naked baby shots are classic. They are wonderful for showing the innocence of the baby (by showing her with no clothes) as well as for showing off the baby's beautiful smooth skin. We do have a rule in our studio that if you're over two years old you keep your clothes on. Two and under is great for naked baby shots. Other than that, the clothes stay on.

•Composition

The real success of this photo comes mainly from the composition. Furthermore, the success lies in the subtlety. The baby's head is placed in a frame that is formed by the darker pillow in the background. This frame prevents your eye from wandering away from the baby's face. Your look pauses on the face of the baby because it is contained by the frame made up of the fringes of the darker pillow.

•Setting and Light

This is one of our simplest set-ups. On the floor is a soft rug, piled with lots of pillows. It's always a good idea to place a waterproof lap pad under babies in case of accidents. We lower the softboxes as far as they would go and tilt them downward to give a soft, controlled light that flatters any subject. Using the strobes is great with moving kids since it tends to freeze their action.

Camera: Canon EOS
Lens: 35-135mm zoom
Film: Kodak TMX 100

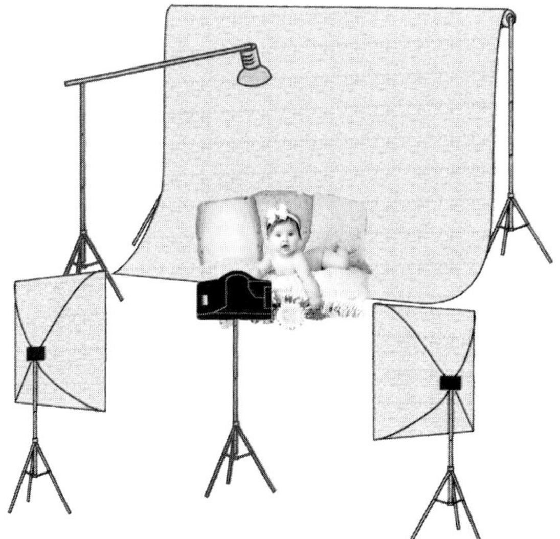

The main light for this shot comes from a softbox placed to the left of the camera. Another softbox is used at half-power from the right side of the camera to provide fill light. A hair light was added above the subject on a boom.

•Repeat Business

It's a privilege to be able to photograph the new members of a family as it grows. In doing a lot of children's photography we get the honor of shooting younger siblings. We establish a good relationship with our clients so that they regularly bring back their children to us to have them photographed.

"... we get the honor of shooting younger siblings."

This is the younger brother of a boy that we did a portrait of a few years earlier. He is wearing the same outfit that his brother wore. Along with him, he brought his favorite comforter and special blanket. It is wonderful to preserve in photographs the special things that families hold dear.

•During the Consultation

During the initial consultation, we always try to ask our clients if they have any special clothes or items that belonged to their grandmothers or ancestors. Perhaps there is some special family heirloom that they would like to have included in the portrait. Even if the special object is set off to the side and is not a main element in the photograph, it connects the family to the portrait and makes it so much more special to them.

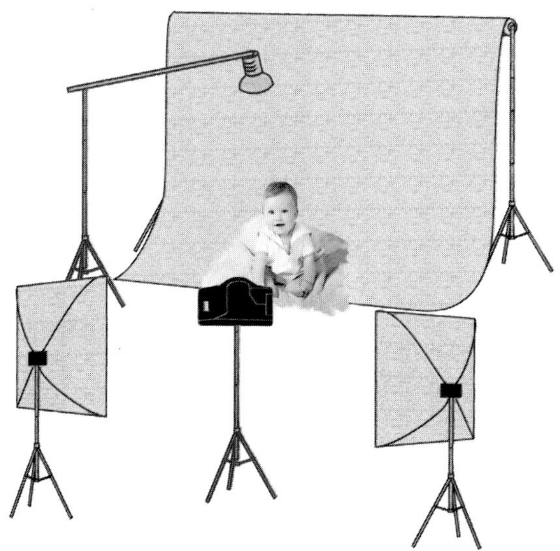

Camera: Canon EOS 630

Lens: 35-135 zoom

Film: Kodak TMX 100, rated at E.I. 80

The main light for this shot comes from a softbox placed to the left of the camera. Another softbox is used at half-power from the right side of the camera to provide fill light. A hair light was added above the subject on a boom.

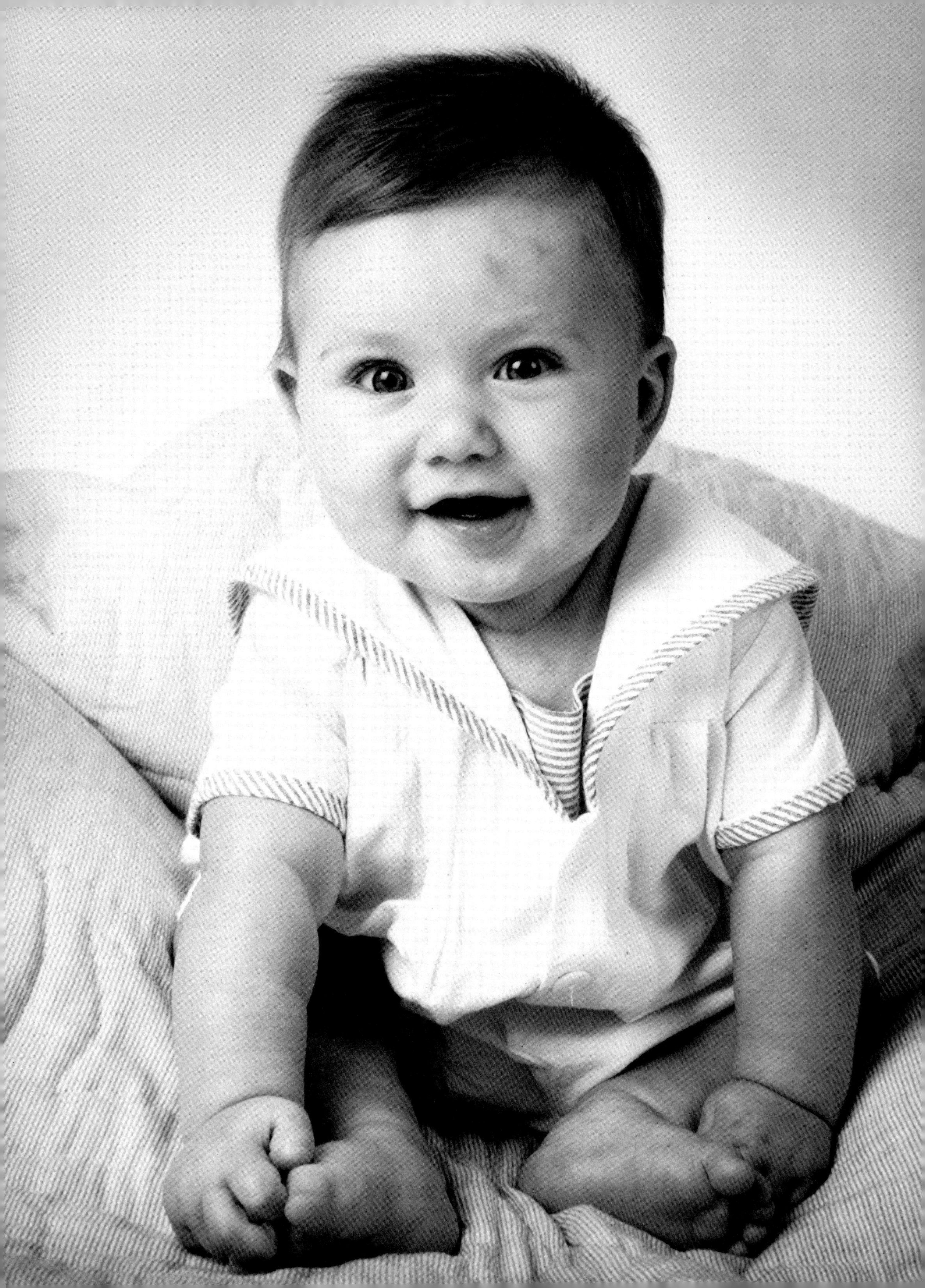

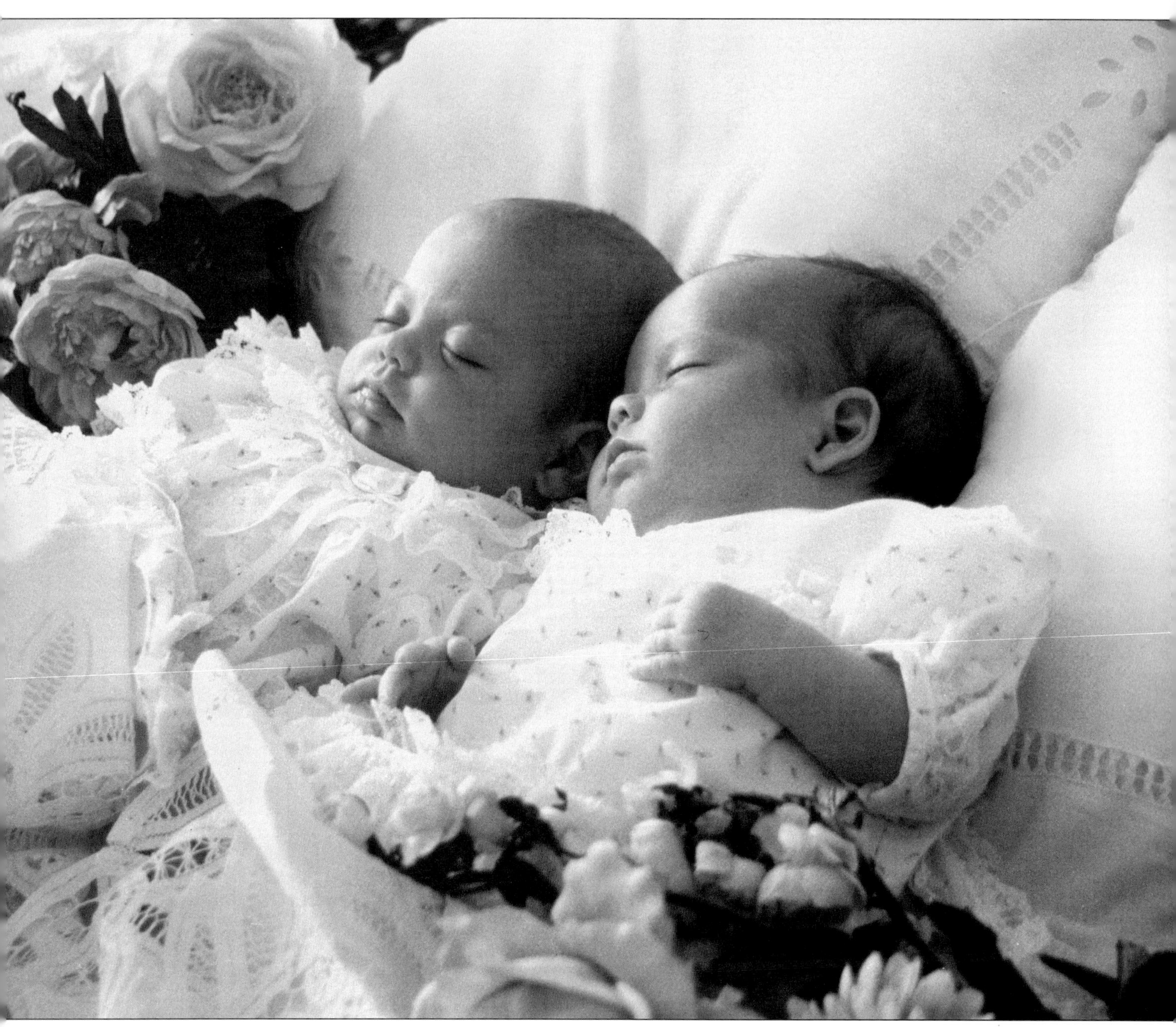

"... twins are just the icing on the cake."

•Twins

There is nothing cuter than a sleeping baby, except perhaps *two* sleeping babies – and twins are the icing on the cake.When babies are only a few weeks old they sleep a lot, and won't stay awake for long. We try to capture them while they are awake, but they can't always make it through the whole shoot.

•Lighting

Here, the lighting is all natural window light. The portrait is slightly back-lit so that the light has a specular quality and skims across the babies' faces to mold their features. We used a big reflector panel to bounce some light into the shadows. The babies are posed in a nest of lacy pillows and blankets with some flowers laid on the ground.

•Down on the Floor

We prefer to shoot babies and young children on the floor instead of on a platform so there's no danger of falling. Sometimes we make a "baby nest" in a chair by stuffing it with oversized pillows and making a little pocket we can "wedge" the baby into. This works well for small infants who aren't able to move around enough to squirm and fall out of the chair. Regardless of age, we always have one parent just out of the camera frame as a "spotter" just in case the baby starts wriggling too much.

Camera: Canon RT

Lens: 35-135mm zoom

Film: Kodak TMX 100, rated at E.I. 80

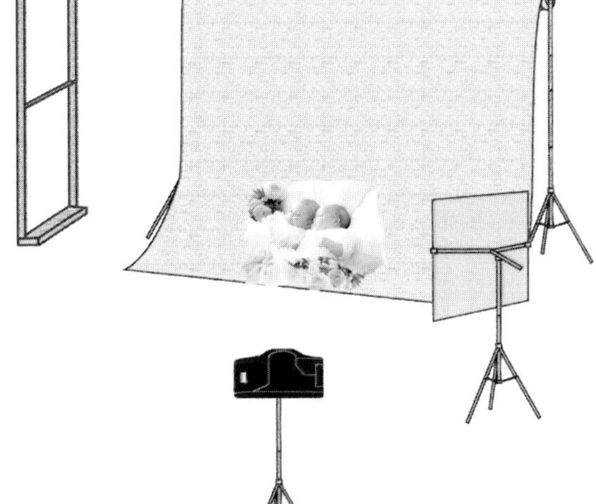

Window light hits the subject from the left, and a translucent panel is used as a reflector to the right of the camera to bounce some light into the shadows.

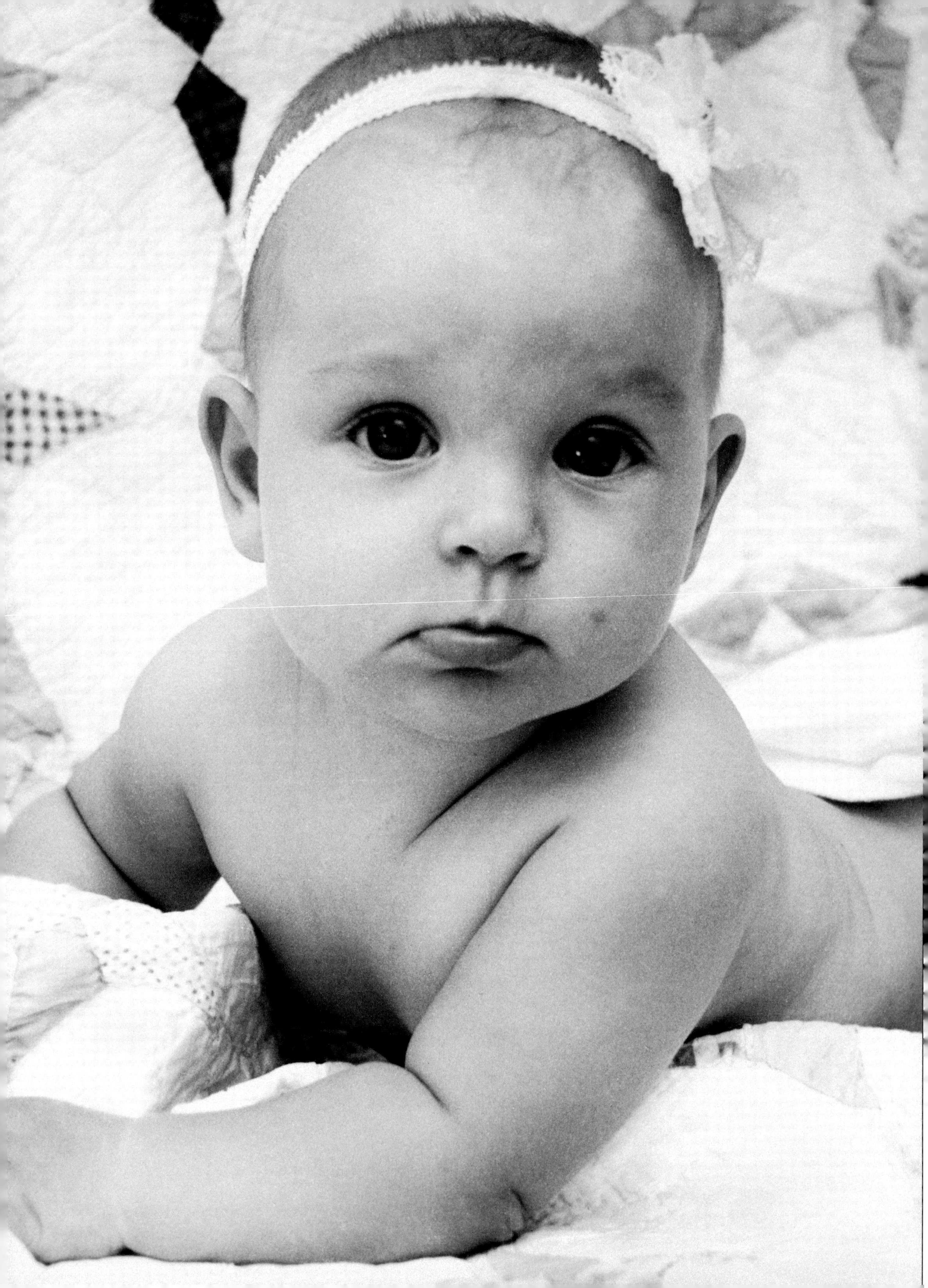

"... to catch kids in motion you need the speed of strobe lighting."

•Lighting

The image was shot using and combination of bounce light and directional light. We took the on-camera flash unit and pointed it up to bounce the light off the ceiling. This accounts for the flat, enveloping light on the baby. This is a good type of lighting to use if you are going to handcolor a photograph with oils.

We also had a separate, bigger strobe set to fire on a slave. The on-camera flash set off the bigger strobe which shone through a big translucent panel set off to the side of the subject.This translucent panel acts like a soft box with a strobe behind it. The strobe to the side of the subject gives a little more molding of the face and adds a bit more definition than using the bounced light of the flash by itself.

Natural light is beautiful and probably my favorite type of light, but to catch kids in motion you need the speed of strobe lighting. A good lighting system is a real necessity to ensure consistent results.

Camera: Canon FTB

Lens: 50mm Canon f-1.8

Film: Ilford XP2, rated at E.I. 200

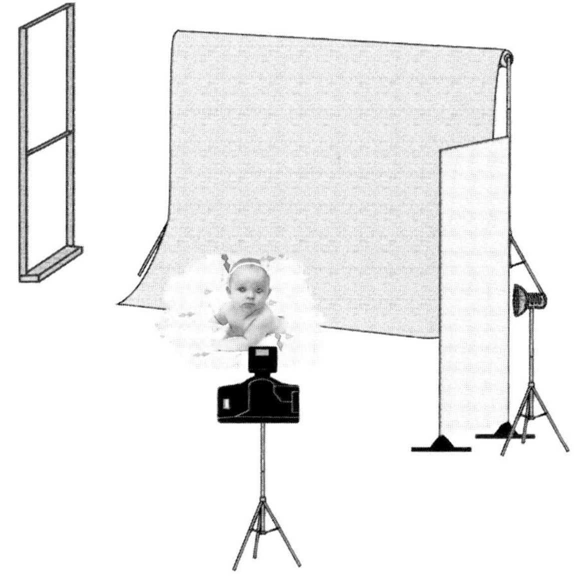

Window light hits the subject from the left. A tungsten light, shot through a diffusion panel, hits the subject from camera right. The final component of the lighting set-up was an on-camera flash.

•Posing

This picture is of a two month old baby. At this age, babies can't yet lay on their stomachs and lift their heads up. Babies at this stage don't even have enough strength or muscle control to sit up or to be held by young siblings. The babies are just too floppy. This means you are limited to shooting them either on their backs, their tummies or being held by an adult.

If you are shooting babies alone on their back, the only way to vary your portraits is to change your camera angle. In this case, we shot a side view as well as a view from directly above looking down on the baby. Obviously, if you shoot at this side angle, you stop at the waist for privacy. Otherwise, you can flip them over and shoot them laying on their tummies.

"... we shot a side view as well as a view from directly above ..."

•Window Light

This shot was taken with available window light late in the day with no fill light or reflectors. The depth of field is very narrow. The baby's front hand is out of focus as is his back hand. This makes you concentrate on looking at the part of the photo which is in sharp focus – in this case, the baby's eyes. This lighting is relatively high contrast but the skin tones are light which sets off the dark eyes of the baby.

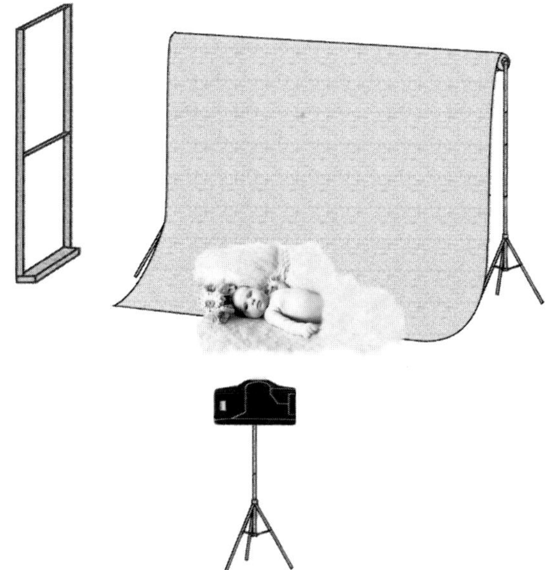

Camera: Canon EOS

Lens: 50mm , f-1.8

Film: Kodak TMX 100, rated at E.I. 80

Window light hits the subject from the left. This is the only source of light used for the portrait.

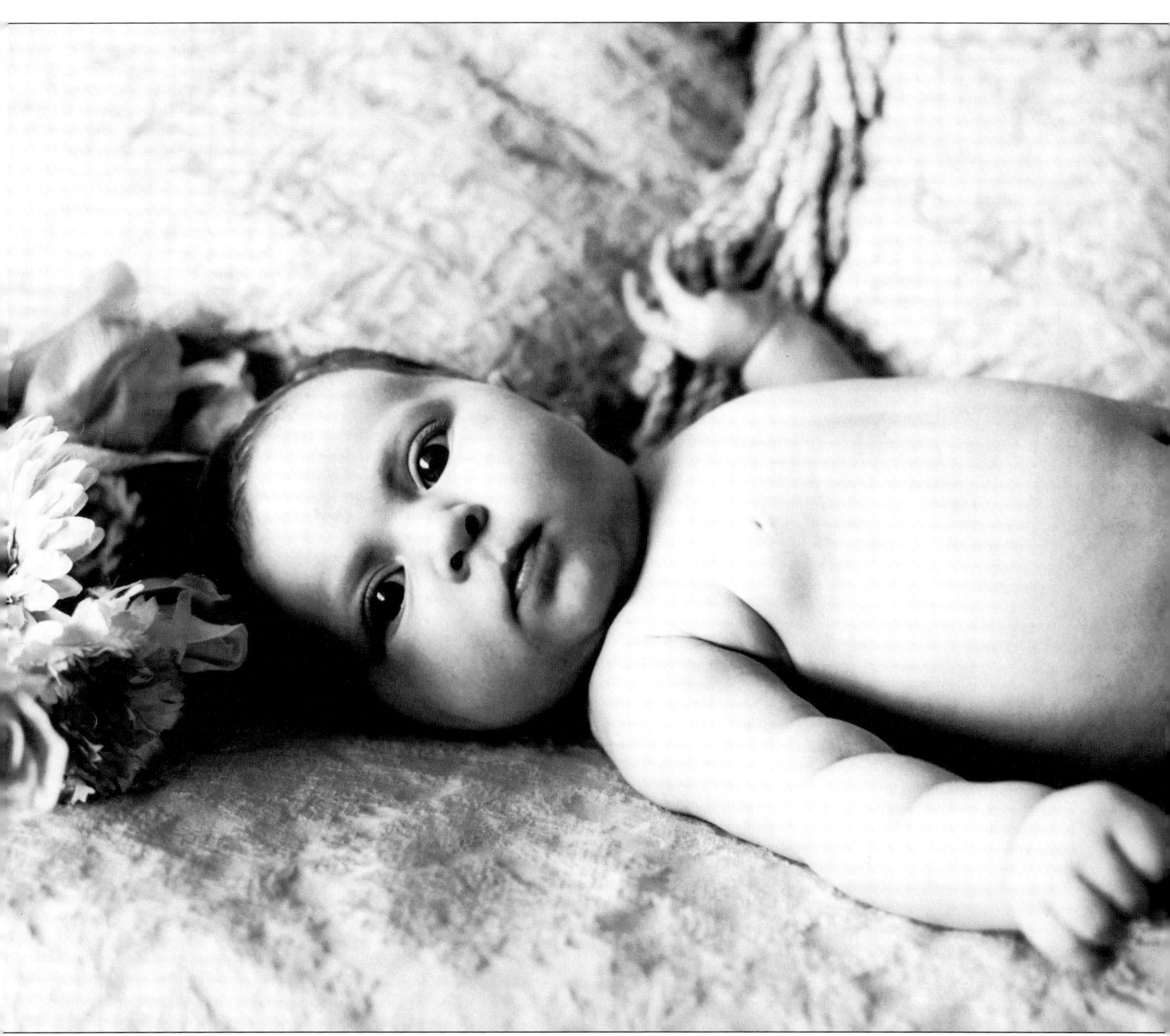

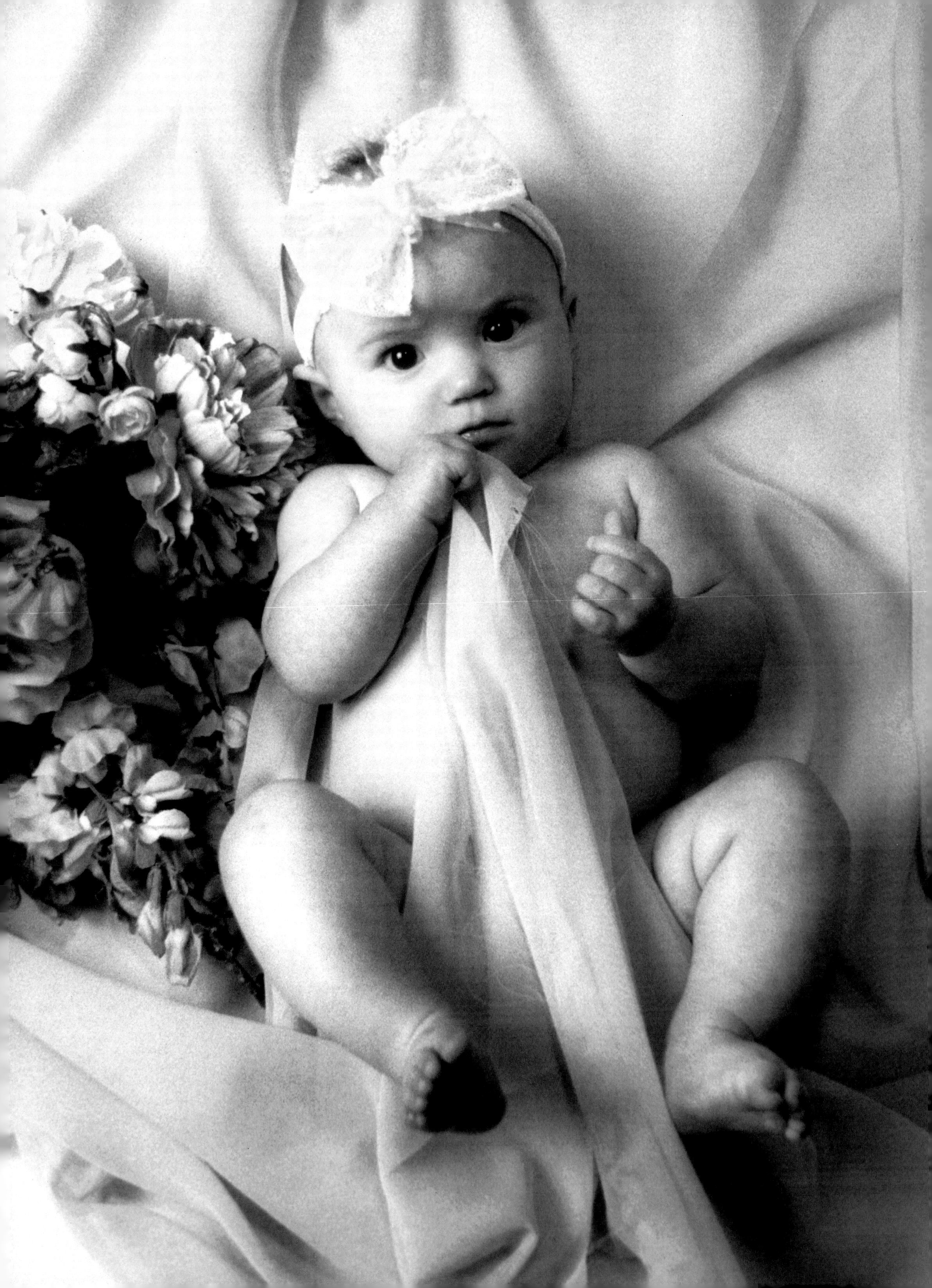

"Make sure to always keep your camera on a neck strap ..."

•Shooting from Above

Standing directly above and shooting down is a great way to photograph small babies. Make sure always to keep your camera on a neck strap so it can't drop down on the baby.

When they are so small that they can't hold up their heads by themselves, we lay babies down on the floor with some sort of material around them. You can use various fabrics, sheer drapes, tablecloths, or any interesting material. We often place flowers near the child for a grounding effect, so it doesn't seem like they are floating in space. Babies have a tendency to pull up their little legs and feet. We give them little flowers or a piece of the material to hold in their hand for modesty.

•Lighting

There is a shift in perception that occurs when you place babies on their backs and shoot them from above. When you hang the photograph on the wall, the babies appear to be floating in space. This photo doesn't look that way because of the lighting. If you light the subject so that it looks like normal portrait (with light on one side and shadow on the other) it will appear more normal when hung. The lighting is simple, a hair light, and a main light coming from the left.

Camera: Canon EOS

Lens: 35-135mm zoom

Film: Agfa 100

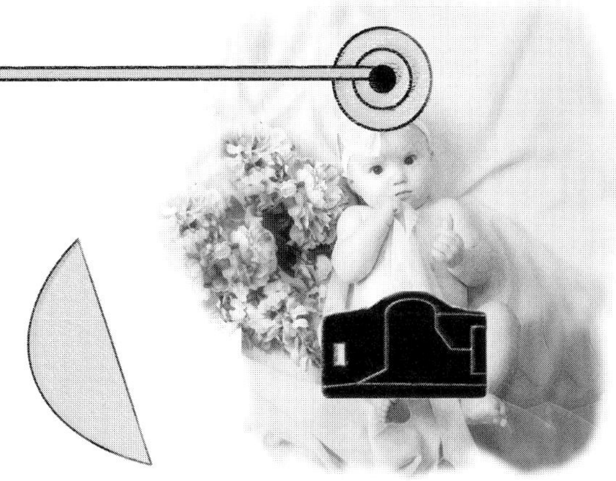

A main light and hair light hit the subject to create a natural-looking light effect when shot from directly above.

•Best Age

We get a lot of calls from people wondering the best age for a baby's first portrait. Unless they are doing a birth announcement, we like to tell people to wait until the baby can lie on its stomach and hold its head up. This usually is somewhere around three to five months old. There is so much more that you can do with infants when they are able to hold their heads up, even just for short periods of time.

•Down on the Floor

We took this picture by laying the baby on the floor and crawling on the floor with her. I was laying on my stomach in order to have the camera at the proper eye level. The mom was right off to the left and talked to the baby so the baby would look right at her.

"We took this picture by laying the baby on the floor and crawling ..."

•High Key Portraiture

For high key portraiture you have to put enough white light on the background to keep it white. We use two Speedotron strobes aimed at the background to keep it white and shadowless. When shooting color you need more light on the background than with black and white, since black and white film has a neutral cast. Because color film can show a color cast it is necessary to blast the background with more light in order to prevent a color cast showing on it.

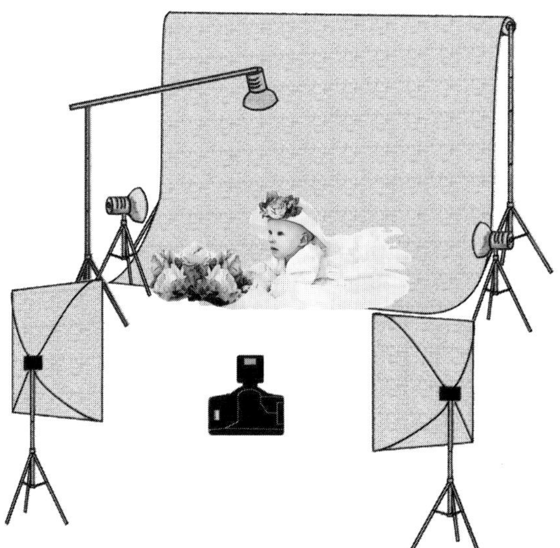

Camera: Canon EOS RT

Lens: 35-135mm zoom

Film: Ilford XP2, rated at E.I. 200

Two softboxes were placed near the camera to either side of the subject. The softbox on the left provided the main light, while the soft box to the right was set at half-power to provide fill light.Two additional lights were used to throw light onto the background. Finally, a hair light was positioned above the subject on a boom.

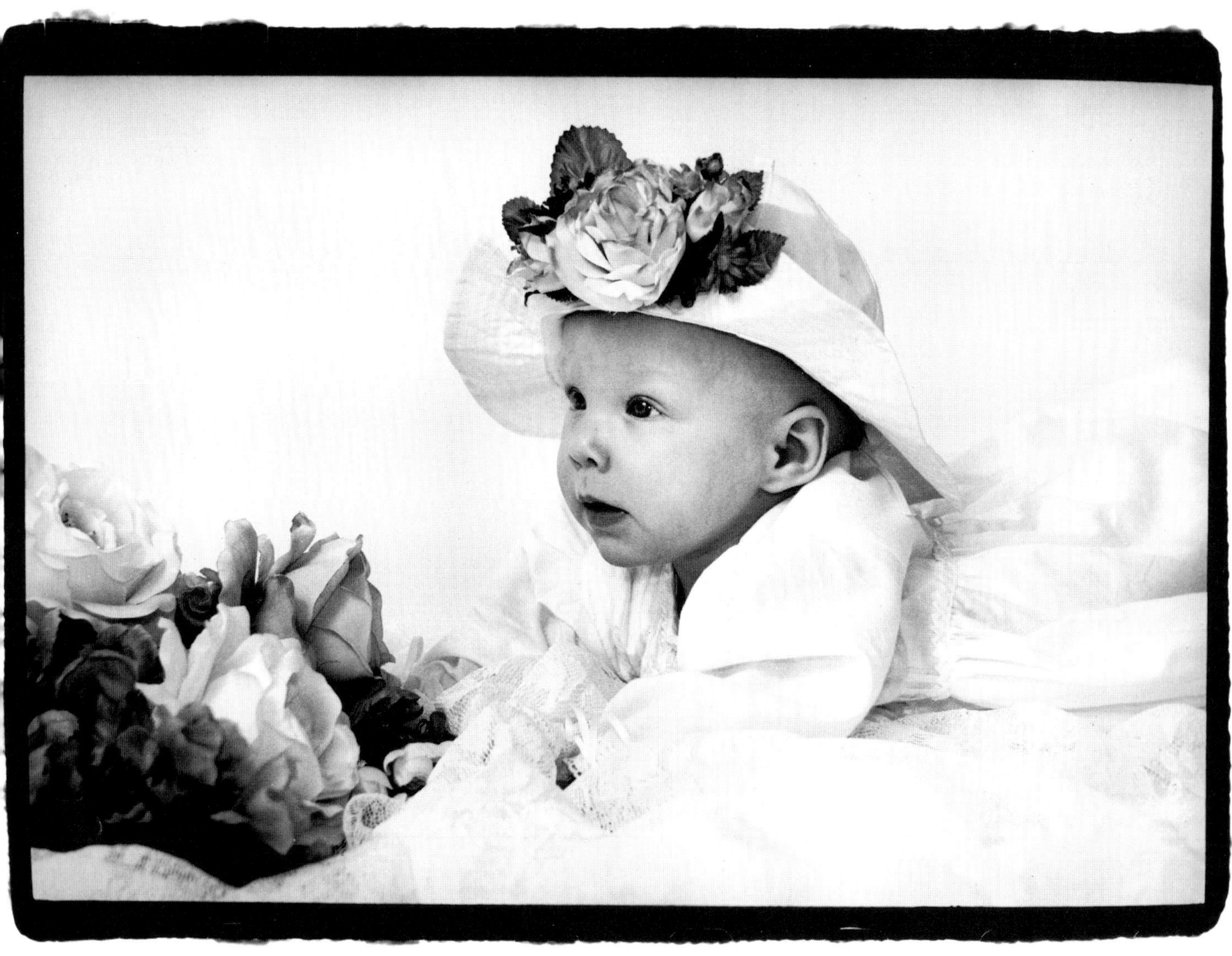

•Posing

This image was shot using natural window light from a northwest facing window. We also used a large white reflector pane to kick in light from the opposite side of the subjects.

•Lighting

We faced the children toward the light so their faces were well illuminated. When there are a small children who can't sit up by themselves it's nice to have an older brother or sister hold the smaller one. We also like to have the parents go outside the window and make faces to get a response out of the children and get them to look out the window.

"We faced the children toward the light ..."

•Composition

The horizontal lines at the bottom of the picture grounds the composition; the vertical ones in the background help to accentuate the verticality of the children. Along the outside edges of the picture we used flowers and leaves to break up the outside edge of the frame. These interrupt the rectangular straight lines that frame the picture and helps to break up the negative space near the corners.

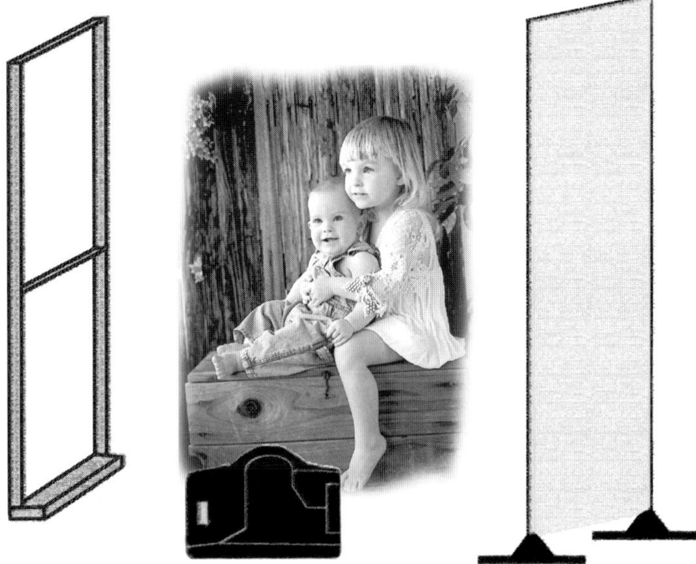

Camera: Canon EOS on tripod
Lens: 50mm Canon f-1.8
Film: Ilford XP2 400 rated at 200

Natural window light illuminates the subjects (who are posed in front of a fence) from camera left. A large reflector panel was used to bounce back some of the window light from the opposite side of the subjects.

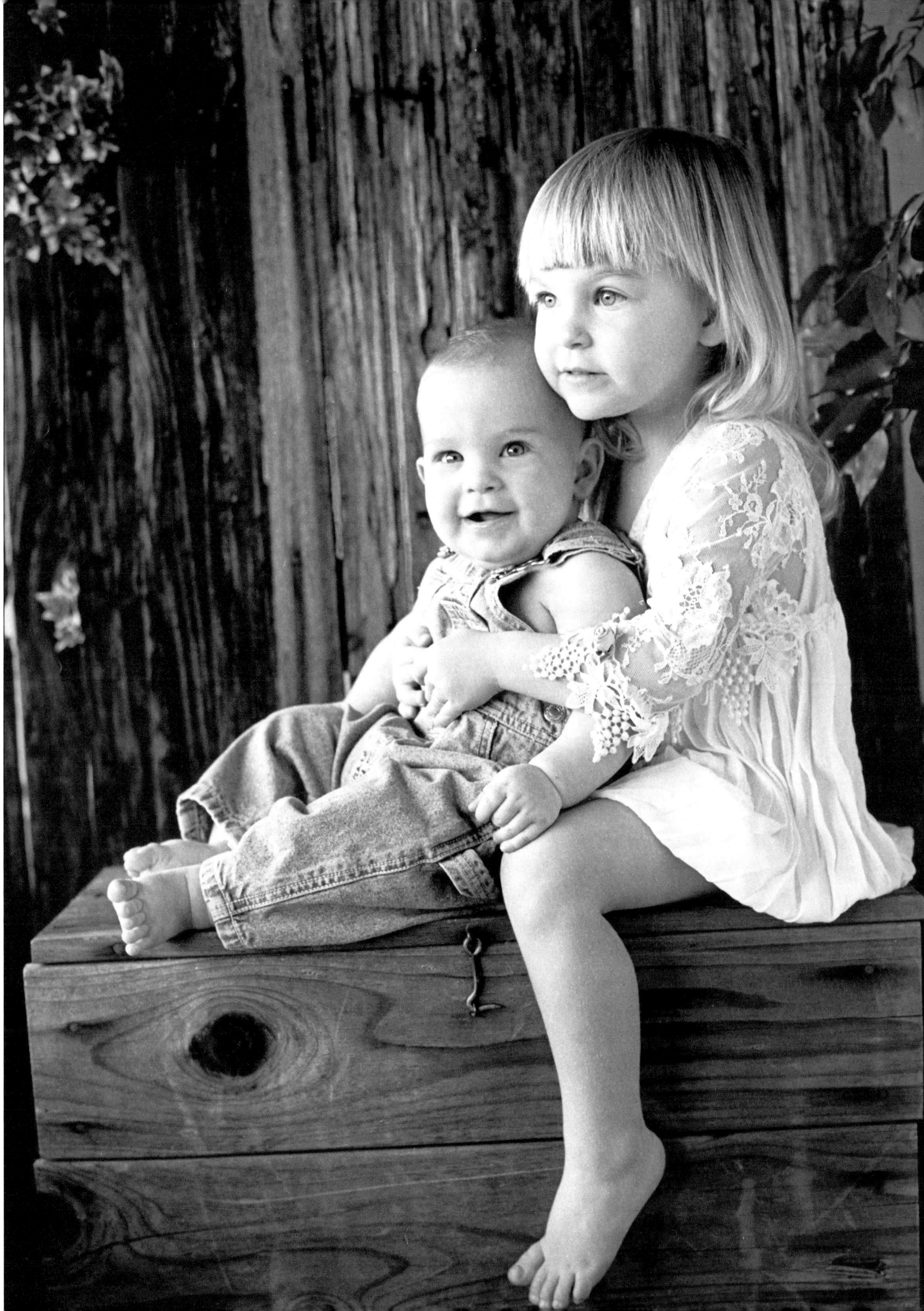

•Entertaining Infants

These babies are at an age (nine months to a year) where they need to be distracted by something or they will be all over the place. Sometimes it is necessary to have parents just outside the frame holding the babies' feet so that they are not flying all around the studio.We also like to distract them with silk flowers or shiny baubles. It is always a good idea to keep you eye on the children or have a parent designated as a spotter so that the children don't find themselves in any kind of hazardous situation.

"We also like to distract them with silk flowers or shiny baubles."

•Composition

Compositionally, there is a circular motif to this photo. Your eye follows around in a circular fashion by traveling around from the faces down to the arm of one of the children and then up the arm of the other child until you reach that point where their heads are touching. Again we have the babies heads together so that there is a physical connection between the two and you can't see light between them. Additionally their heads and arms form the outline of a heart or valentine.

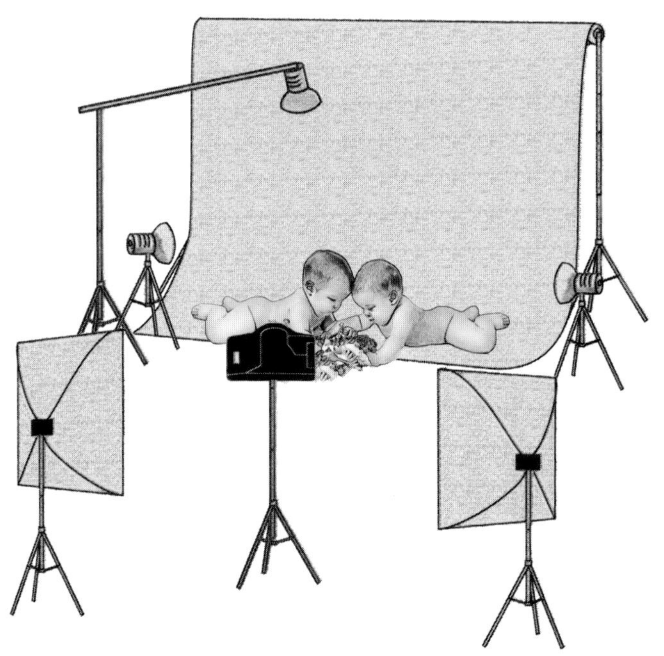

Camera: Canon EOS 630
Lens: 35-135mm zoom
Film: Kodak TMAX CN400, rated at E.I. 200

The photograph was illuminated using five lights. Two softboxes were placed near the camera to either side of the subjects. The softbox on the left provided the main light, while the soft box to the right was set at half-power to provide fill light.Two additional lights were used to throw light onto the background. Finally, a hair light was positioned above the subjects on a boom.

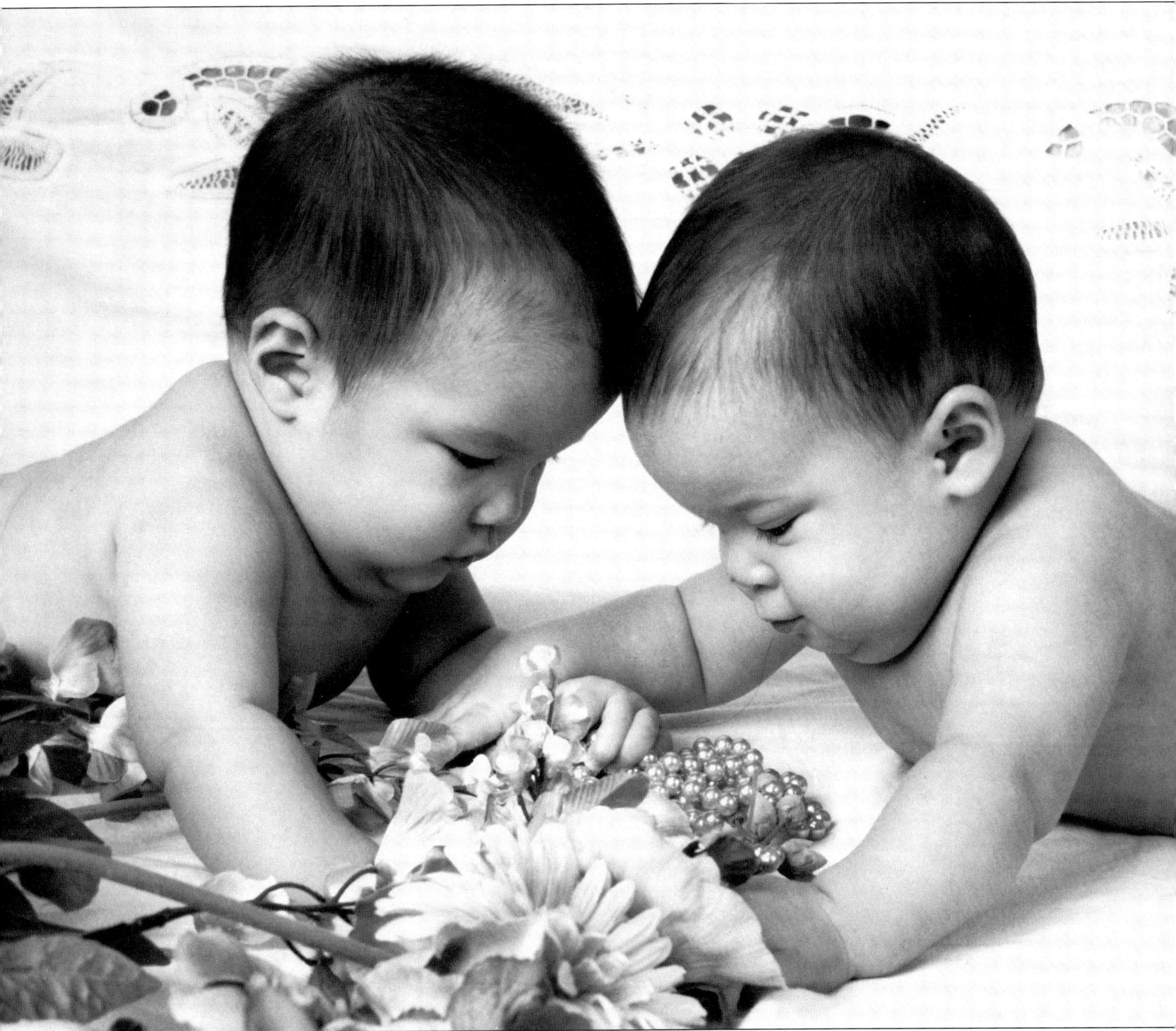

•Using Infrared

Posing infants with parents is a natural. This portrait of a Dad and his newborn son was shot in the studio on infrared film. Instead of using a #25 red filter to block most of the visible light so the film "sees" mostly the infrared spectrum, for portraiture we shoot without a filter. This is because the red filter has a filter factor of about two stops, making the film speed slower than we like for shooting people.

"Posing infants with parents is a natural."

Because the infrared rays focus on a different plane than the visible light rays, the resulting infrared image superimposed over the visible light image is slightly out of focus.That makes the skin tones glow. Because infrared can also "see through" the top layer of skin (which contains more wrinkles and blemishes than deeper layers), it also tends to give the skin a smoother appearance.

One disadvantage of using infrared film in the studio is that some materials reflect more infrared than others. When photographing some clothing, polyester thread (often used in hems and seams) may reflect the infrared while the natural fibers do not. Pure cotton clothing works best when using infrared film.

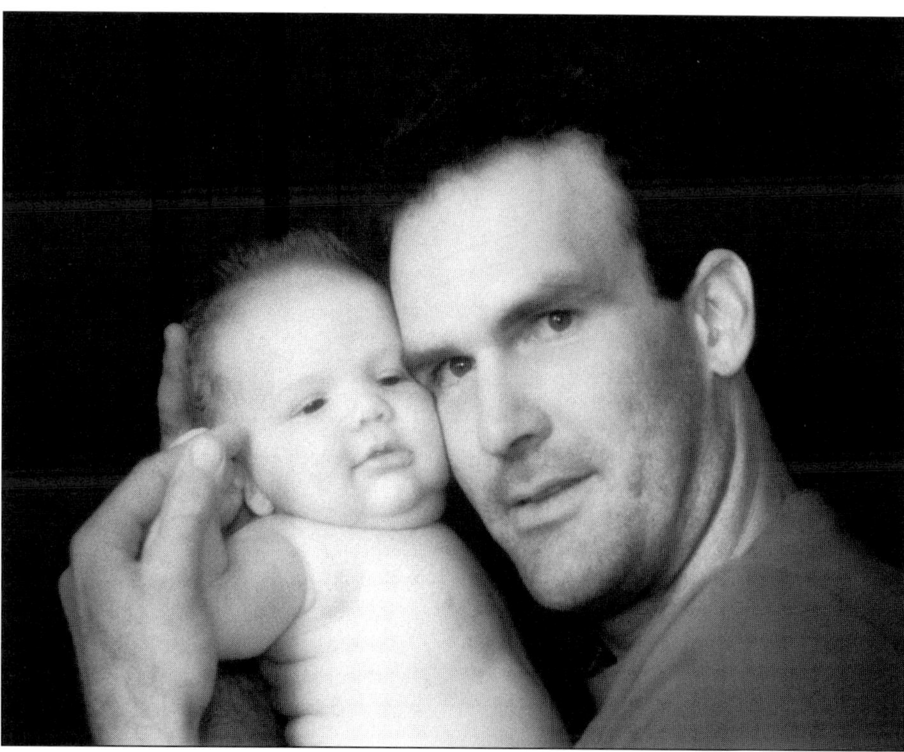

Camera: Canon Eos 630

Lens: 50mm

Film: Kodak high speed infrared, rated at E.I. 80

Filter: none

Kids and Pets

"I love dogs and have always brought them into the studio for family photo sessions. After all, they are part of the family."

•Lighting

The girl's eyes are very sharp and bright and you will notice that her pupils are large. This photo was taken late in the afternoon with natural light through a northwest facing window. We also used some kicker fill light from a reflector off to the right side.

"The girl's eyes are very sharp and bright ..."

•Depth of Field

Because this was taken with natural light there is a particularly narrow depth of field. The foreground focus is just at the dog's nose, which is slightly out of focus – even the hair near the girl's ear is out of focus.

This contrast between the in focus and out of focus areas guides your eye to the object of sharp focus: the girl's eyes, which are wide open and alert. That's right where you want the viewer to look.

•Working with Dogs

In order to get the dog to tip its head like this we have a little plastic squeaker that we use. Give the device a little squeak and the dog automatically tilts its head.

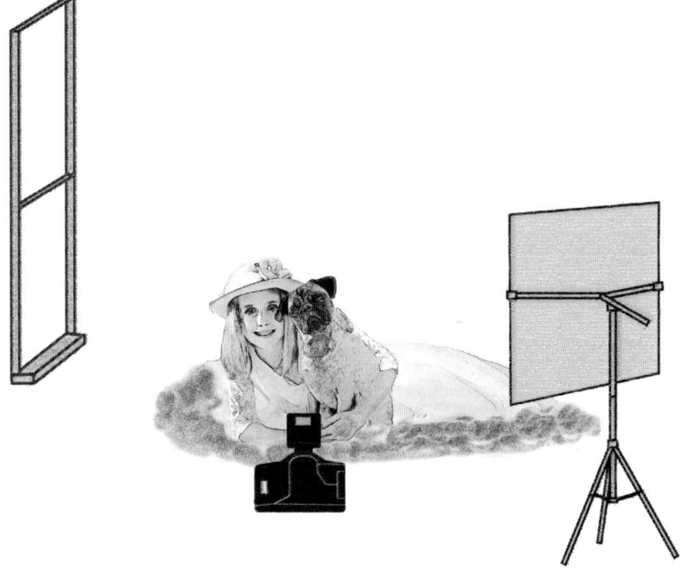

Camera: Canon EOS

Lens: 35-135mm zoom

Film: Ilford XP2, rated at E.I. 200

Natural window light illuminates the subject and her dog from camera left. A reflector was used to bounce back some of the window light from the opposite side of the subjects.

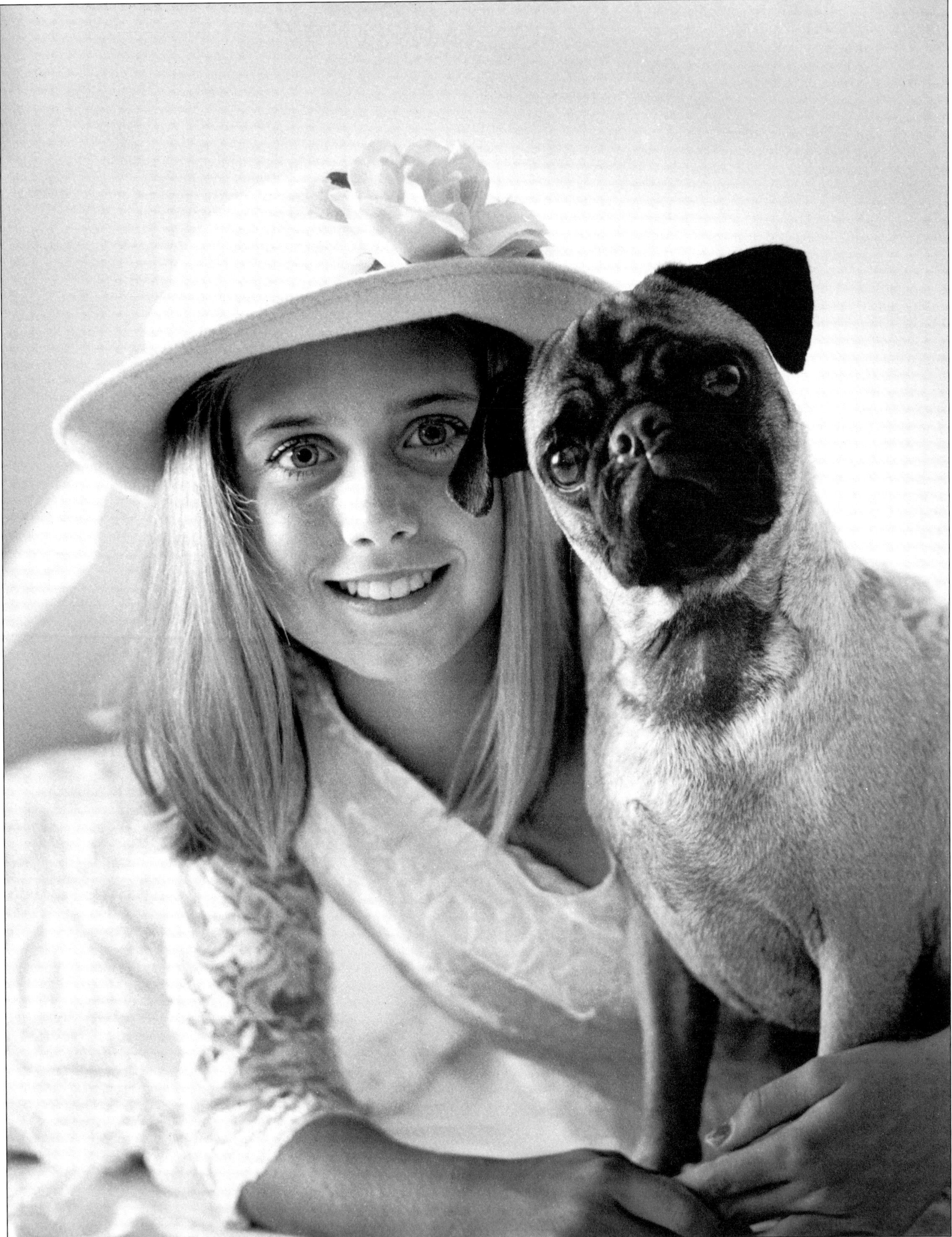

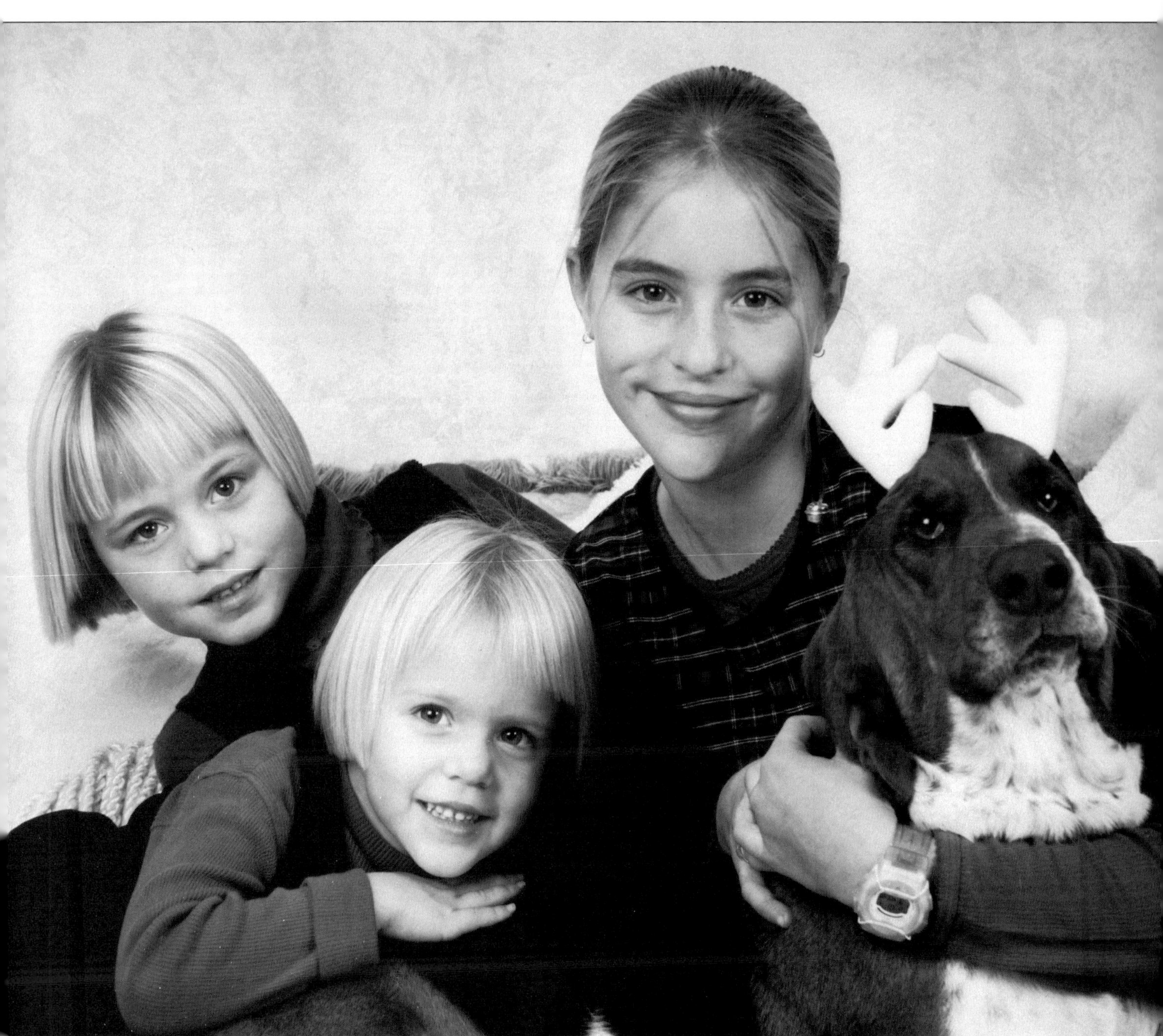

"... youngsters change so fast their first year or two."

•Scheduling Portrait Sessions

Like all studios, our holiday photo sessions are booked from August all the way through the holiday season itself.

When there are very young children in the family, you almost have to wait until October or November to shoot the family, because youngsters change so fast in their first year or two. In families with older children, we can safely shoot earlier in the season so we have time to do all the production work before the big holiday crunch.

•Posing

There is nothing as cute and sad looking as a Basset hound. Truly a family member and loved to death, this dog has it made. The girls did a great job of keeping him still and maintaining their own poses.

Camera: Canon EOS RT

Lens: 35-135mm zoom

Film: Kodak TMAX 100 rated at E.I. 80

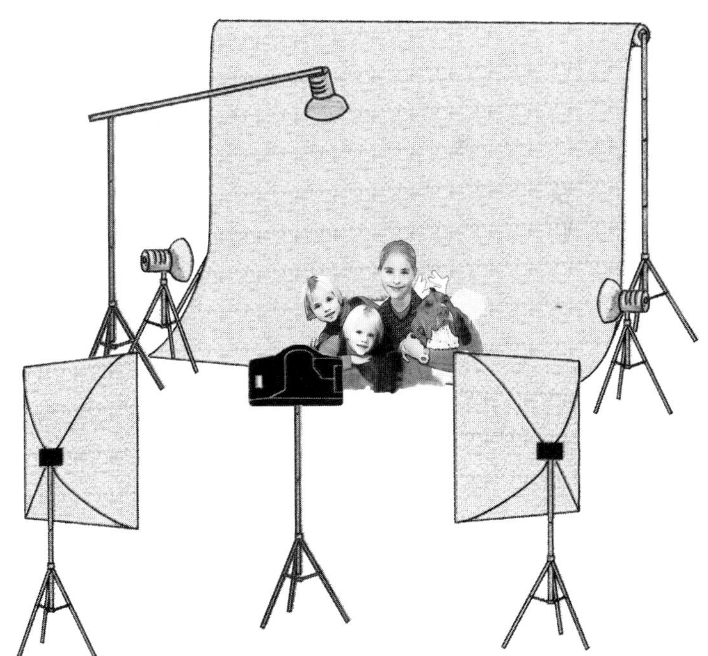

The photograph was illuminated using five lights. Two softboxes were placed near the camera to either side of the subjects. The soft-box on the left provided the main light, while the soft box to the right was set at half-power to provide fill light. Two additional lights were used to throw light onto the background. Finally, a hair light was positioned above the subjects on a boom.

•Dog Behavior

I love dogs and have always brought them into the studio for family photo sessions. After all, they are part of the family. Not all dogs will behave as well as this one, but they all respond to noises. For this shot, my assistant squeaked a door in the back of the studio to make the dog look up. We also ask the family if there are any key words that make their dogs perk up like, "walkie," a special name for treats, or a nickname that they have for the dog. If all else fails just call out, "Here Kitty, Kitty."

"After all, they are part of the family."

•Posing on the Floor

I was laying on the studio floor so that I could be at the right camera angle to take this shot. I asked the kids to get real close to the dog to keep him still. When kids are down flat on the ground like this you must watch to see if their feet are visible over their heads (we call them bunny ears). Just ask them to keep their feet low on the ground. You may also notice that laying down on white seamless paper reflects up some light on their faces.

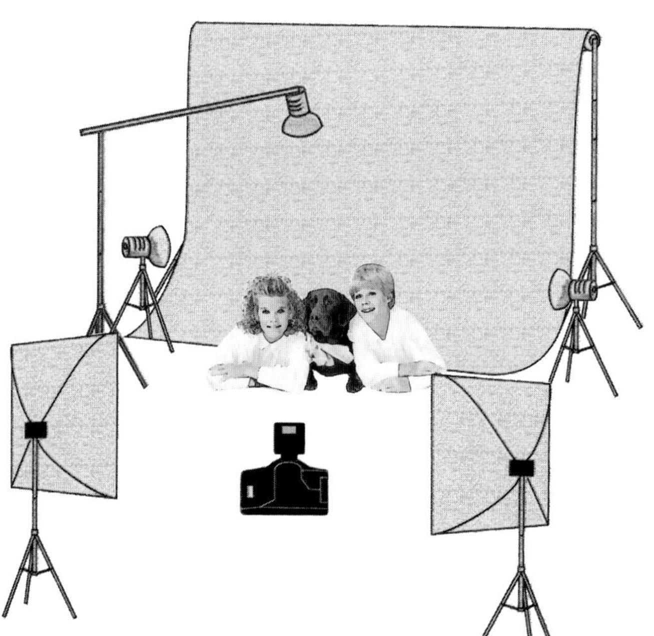

Camera: Canon EOS

Lens: 50mm, f-1.8

Film: Ilford XP1, rated at E.I. 200

The photograph was illuminated using five lights. Two softboxes were placed near the camera to either side of the subject. The softbox on the left provided the main light, while the soft box to the right was set at half-power to provide fill light. Two additional lights were used to throw light onto the background. Finally, a hair light was positioned above the subjects on a boom.

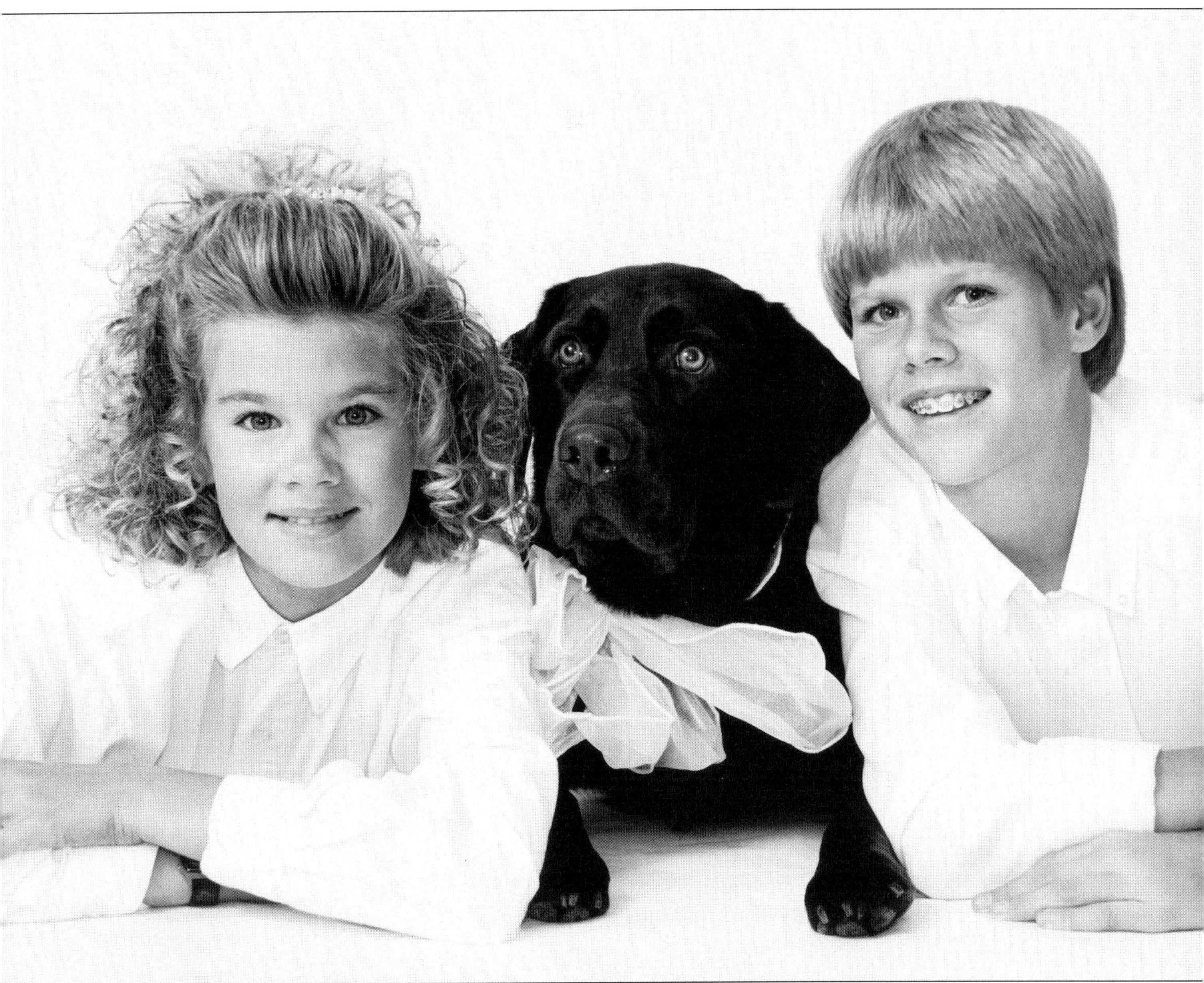

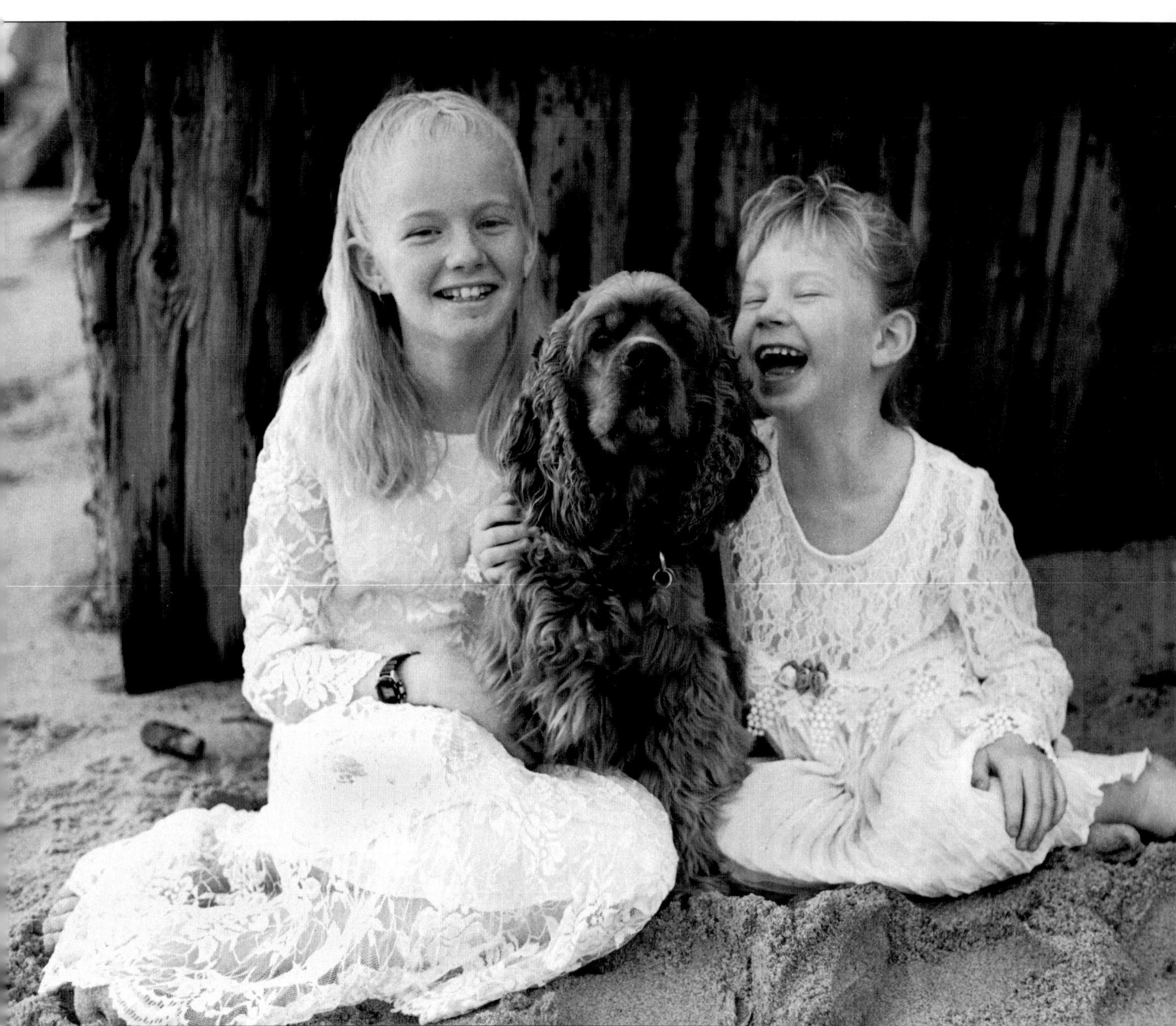

"... check with your local parks and recreation department ..."

•Pets on Location

Pets are part of the family and it's important to include them in the portrait. Most of the time there is no problem taking a pet to the beach or park for a portrait sitting. You should check with your local parks and recreation department or police department to find out the rules for animals in public places. Always keep pets on a leash and make sure to clean up after them so the area is clean for the next person.

•Clothing

The dresses that the girls are wearing are studio props. We use a lot of these cream colored dresses and carry them in sizes from 2 to 12. Not everyone likes to wear the studio clothing but it helps when someone is in a bind and doesn't know what to wear. We also have a whole trunk full of cream colored sweaters in different sizes, because you occasionally get someone who is wearing their favorite tartan plaid shirt. In this case, it becomes necessary to steer them toward a solid color sweater so they can blend in with the group.

It's important to have an initial clothes consultation with your clients so mistakes like that don't happen. Still, they will happen occasionally and you should be prepared for them.

Camera: Canon EOS 630

Lens: 35-135 zoom

Film: Ilford XP2, rated at E.I. 200

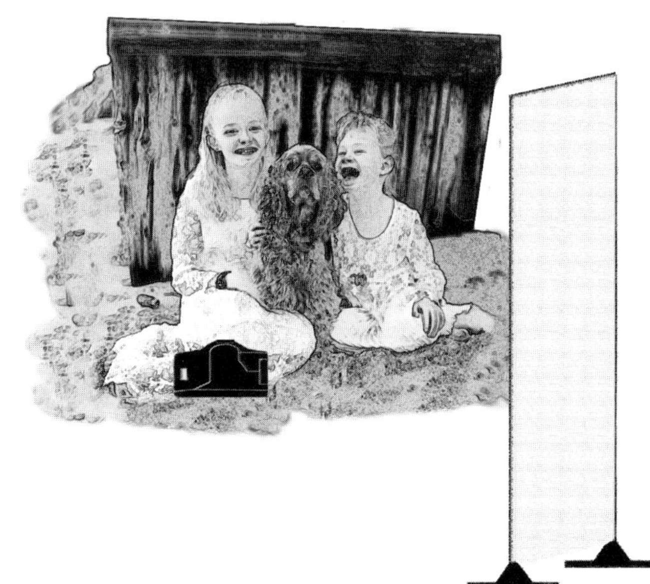

Natural sunlight illuminates the subjects from camera left. A large reflector panel was used to bounce back some of the light from the opposite side of the subjects.

•Birds

They may not be "pets," but wild birds make wonderful props, and kids love to feed them. We always try to have a loaf of day old bread for the kids to feed to the birds. In the park, pigeons and other birds will gather as the kids throw out bird seed. The birds can serve a dual purpose by giving the kids something fun to do, and providing interesting elements in the composition of the photograph.

"... wild birds make wonderful props, and kids love to feed them."

•Making it Look Natural

This is a simple but elegant portrait of a brother and sister walking on the beach. Whenever we shoot people walking away from the camera we try to catch the action of the feet so that the toes are still on the ground and the heel is lifted up off the ground. Making sure that both feet are on the ground makes the subjects look balanced. When their heels are raised you get the impression that they are really walking and not just posing.

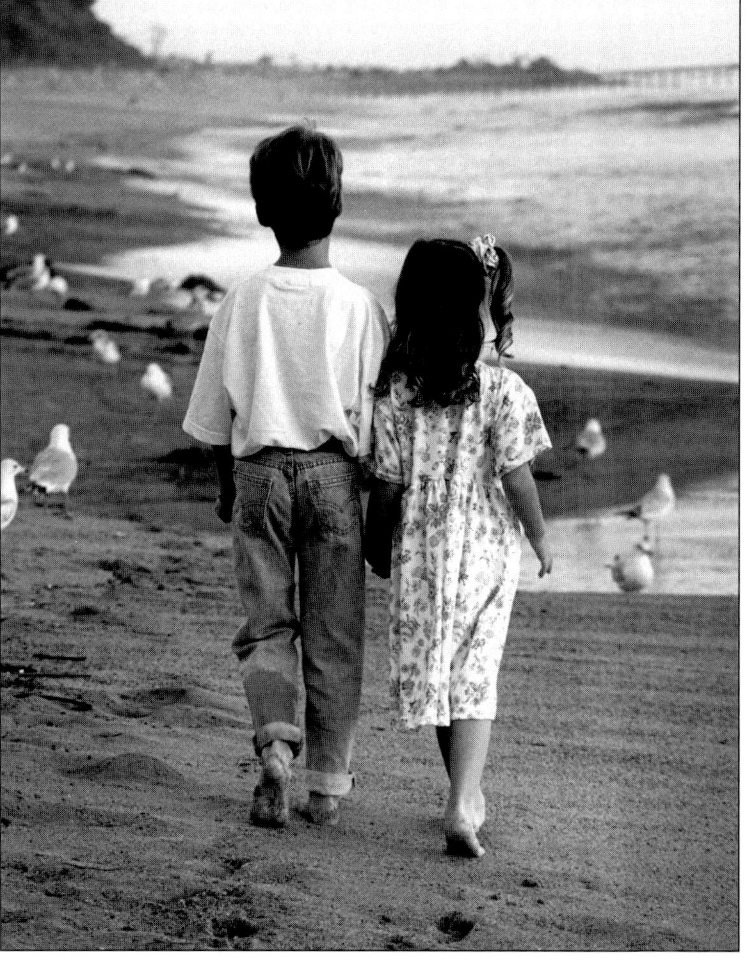

Camera: Canon EOS

Lens: 35-135mm zoom

Film: Ilford XP2, rated at E.I. 200

LOCATION PORTRAITS

"No matter what your neighborhood looks like, it just takes a little footwork to find some unique locations where you can shoot."

•A Glimpse of Childhood

It may seem crazy to take a portrait where you can't see the subjects faces. Isn't the whole idea to capture the appearance of someone so that when you look at the photograph it triggers a memory of that person at that age, or at that point in his or her life? Sometimes it's better not to show faces. Instead of conveying the image of another person and bringing to mind the memory of that person, a photo of seemingly anonymous people allows you to put yourself into the picture. In doing so you can extract emotion from the scene that is singularly yours.

"Sometimes it's better not to show faces."

This portrait is more of a glimpse of childhood than it is a picture of two particular girls on the beach. It summons up the feeling of best friends, and what it meant to have a best friend when you were a child.

•Composition

Elements of composition are sometimes ones that you struggle with consciously, other times the answers come intuitively. The more you shoot the more intuitive your technique becomes.

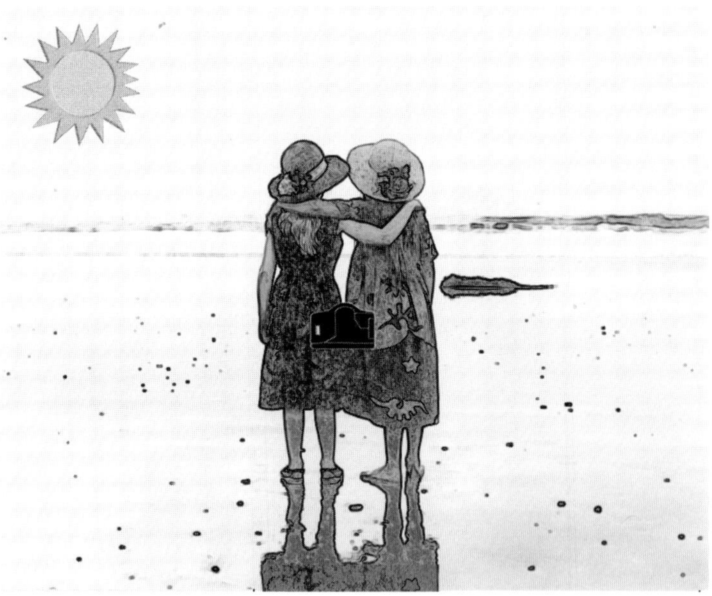

Camera: Canon EOS RT

Lens: 35-135mm zoom

Film: Kodak TMAX, rated at E.I. 80

Sunlight illuminates the subjects from camera left. The photo was shot from the back to capture something of the essence of childhood, rather than just the appearance of these particular girls.

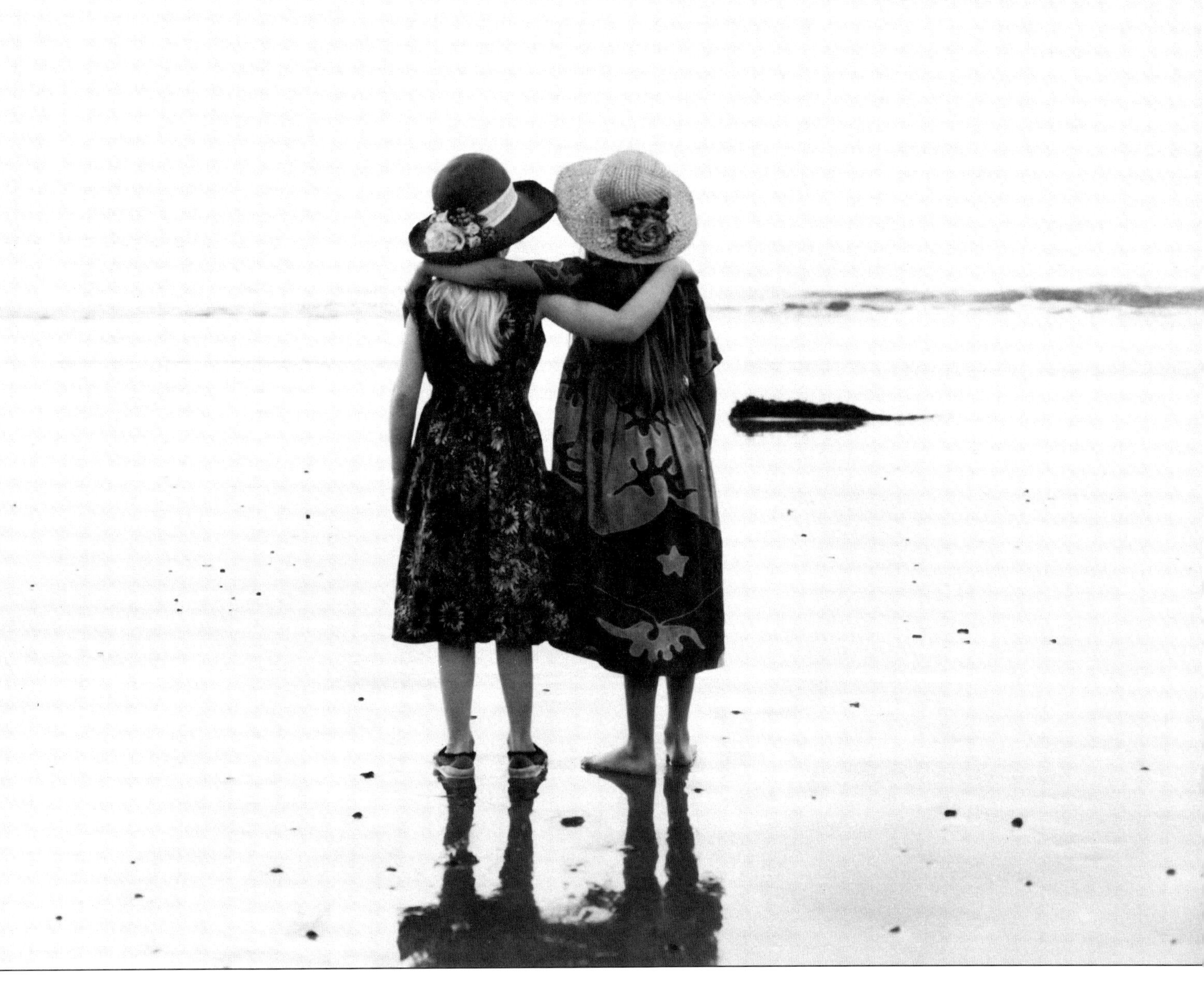

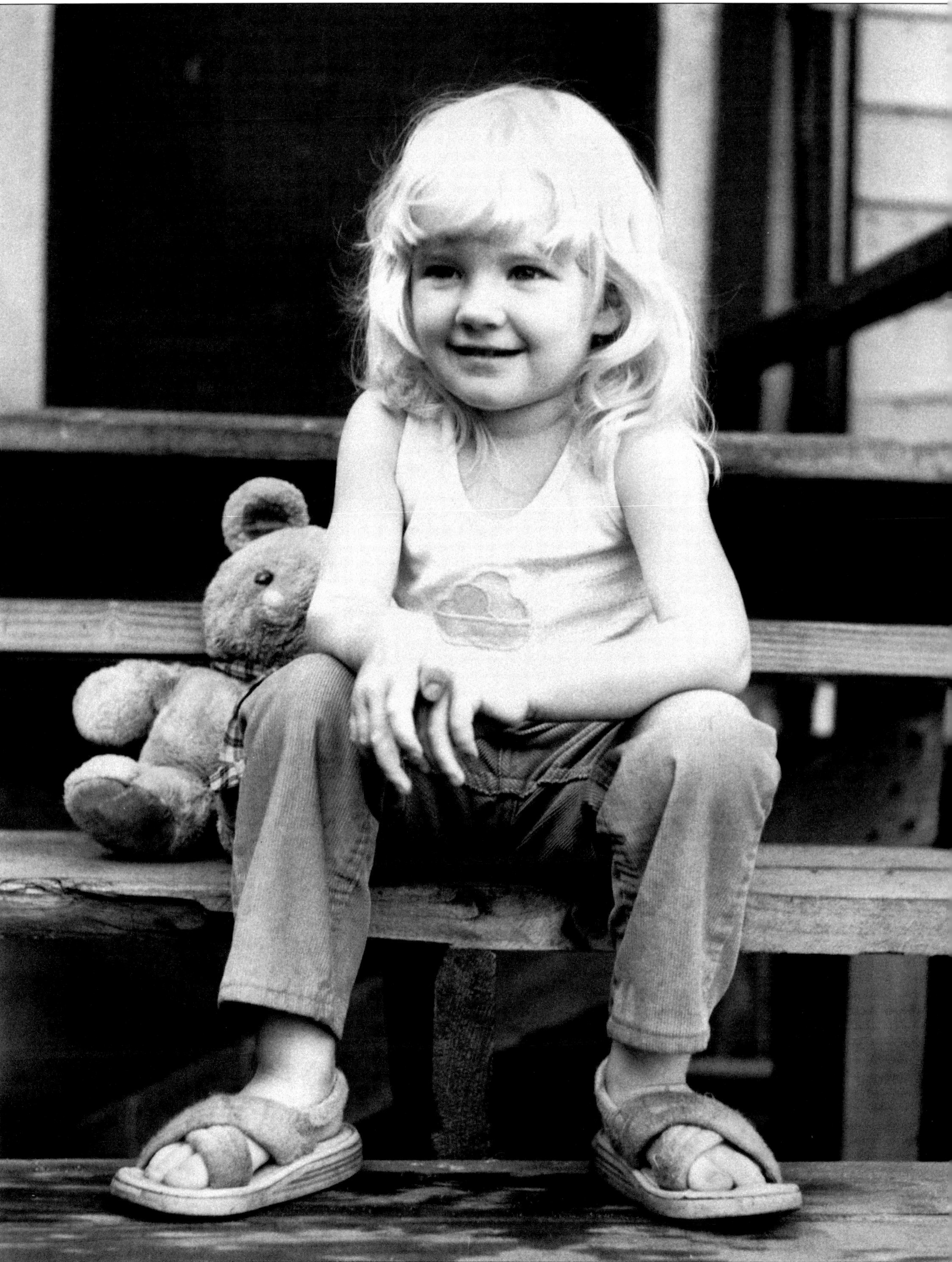

•Lighting

This portrait was shot entirely with natural light – no flash, no fill, just soft natural light. The day was somewhat overcast so there were no harsh shadows. The girl was posed in the shadow of a building.

•Talking with Kids

"... it makes the whole session glide along more smoothly."

When you sit down with a child and start talking before you begin shooting, you develop a rapport with the child and it makes the whole session glide along more smoothly. At some point, as your experience increases, you'll find you're able to talk and shoot at the same time without missing a beat.

Topics of conversation can spring up from the setting itself (for instance, you could talk about that little bear in the background of this image). Kids also like to talk about their friends, their pets, favorite toys and anything else that interests them. If you can get kids to talk about themselves they will forget that you have a camera aimed at them. Getting your subject to feel comfortable and at ease will pay off in better images.

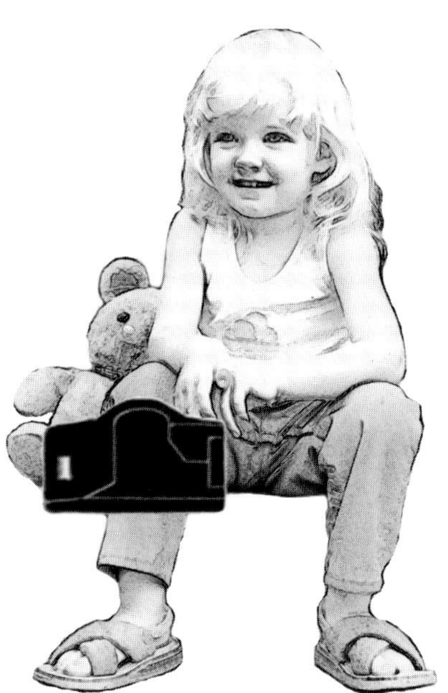

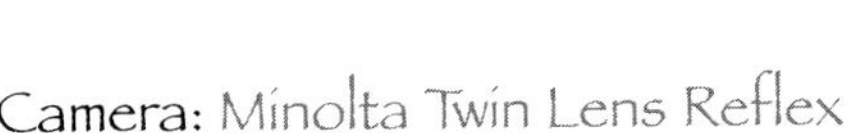

Camera: Minolta Twin Lens Reflex

Lens: 80mm

Film: Kodak PlusX, rated at E.I. 125

Sunlight illuminates the subject from camera right. The sky was overcast, providing soft, diffuse light and the subject was posed in the shade of a building.

•Morning Light

I love gray foggy mornings when the light envelopes everything with a soft diffusion. It's one of my favorite times of the day. But like most things, early morning at the beach is unpredictable. Sometimes you have to take a "wait and see" attitude. Depending upon the time of year, you can be greeted by bright light or overcast skies.

"It's one of my favorite times of the day."

•Squinting

On this particular morning, we were greeted by bright sun. Under these circumstances we have to be watchful that our clients don't squint too much. One technique that we use is to have the people close their eyes tight and tilt their faces up to the sun making sure to keep their eyes tightly closed. This "pre-exposure" to the brightness of the sun allows them to be less squinty when they open their eyes.

•Fill Light

We almost always use some sort of fill light on a bright day. Either fill flash or reflector will provide enough light to open up the shadows.

•Printing

This shot is printed in vignette format to eliminate some of the distracting background.

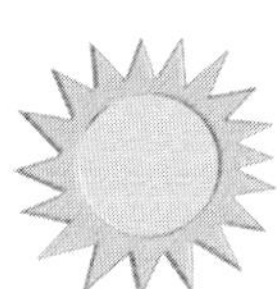

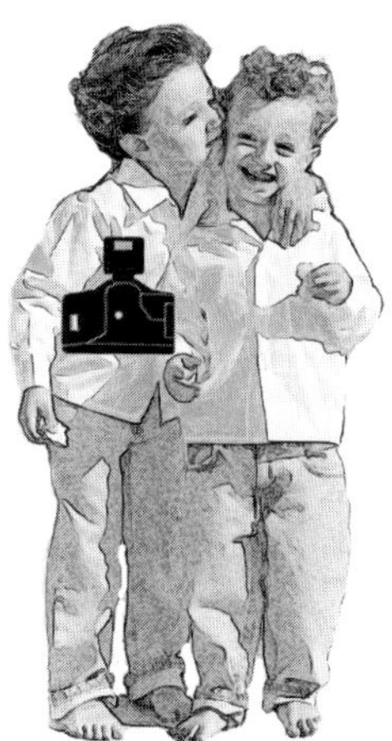

Camera: Canon EOS

Lens: 35-135mm Canon zoom

Film: Ilford XP2, rated at E.I. 200

The main light source for this image was the bright sunlight from camera right. A flash was added on-camera to provide fill light and open up the shadows on the subjects' faces.

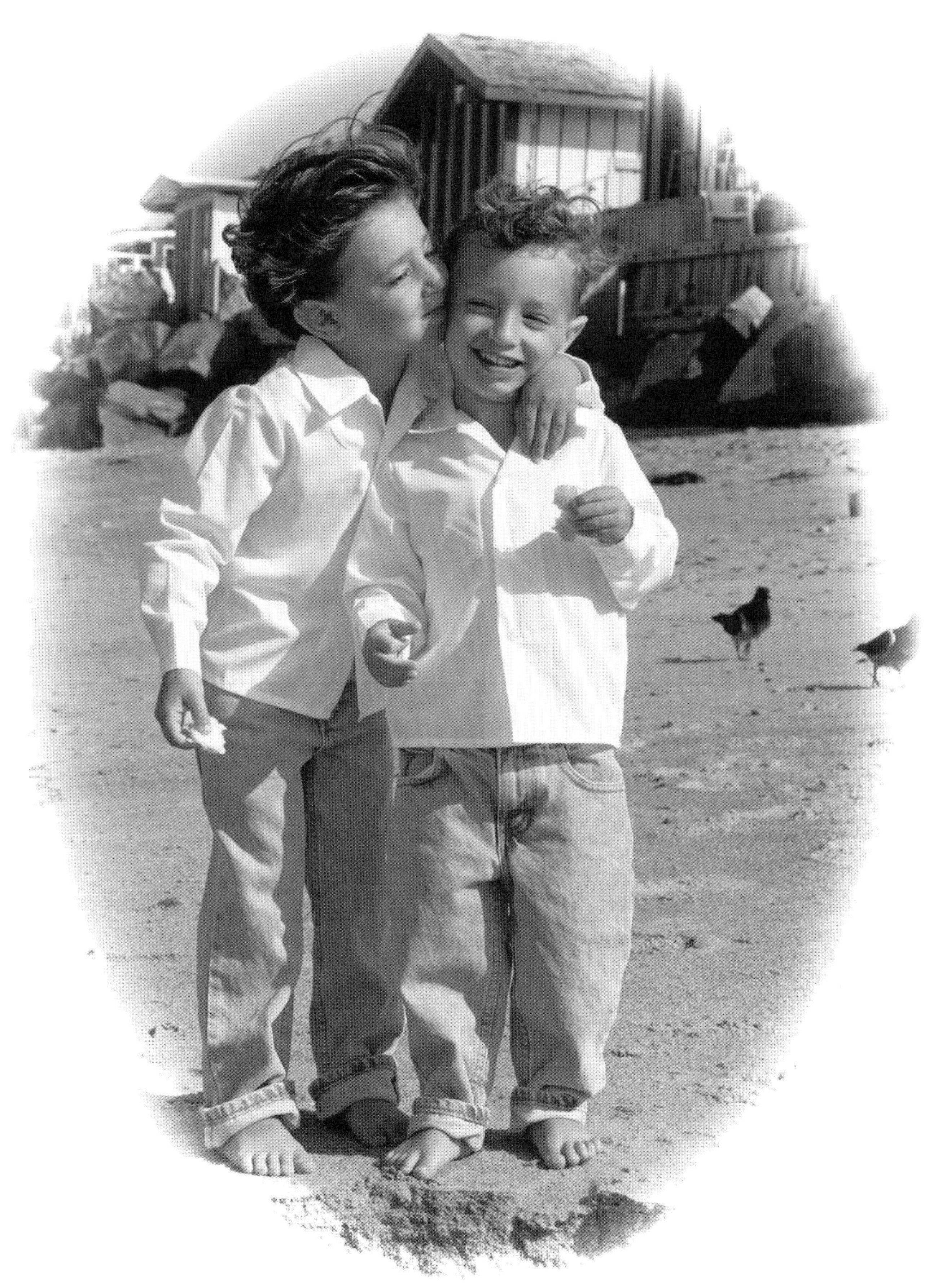

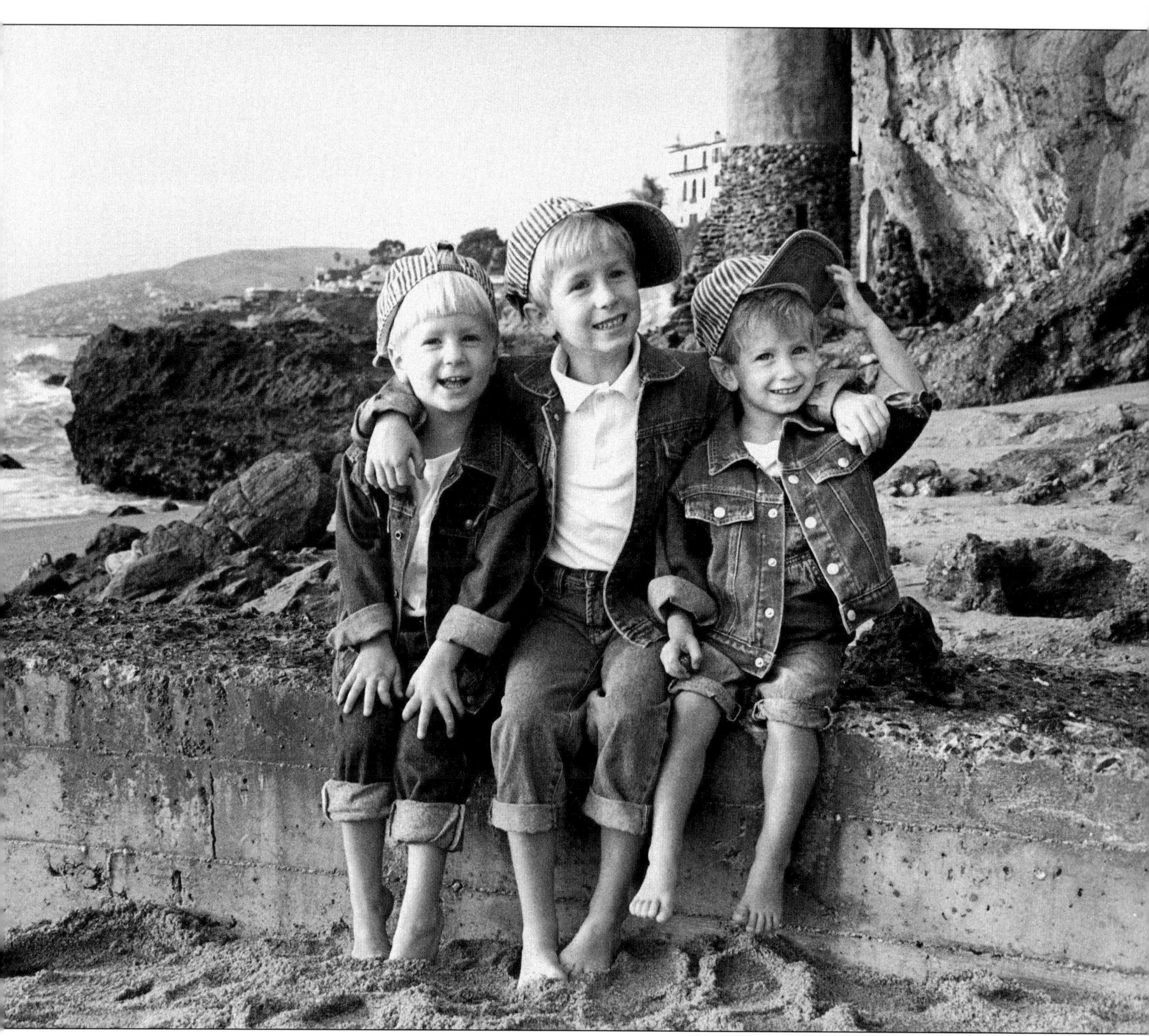

"... they're ready to have a good time."

•Kids will be Kids

When kids get to the beach they're ready to have a good time. It's natural for kids to want to get up and run around. Just keeping their hats on is a trick (in fact, when you get a cute shot of a child holding on to his hat it's probably because he's about to take it off).

•An Assistant

You just can't overestimate the value of having a good assistant to settle down those active kids. Playing with them (or having your assistant play with them) helps ensure you'll get a photograph that portrays their personalities.

•Lighting

The fill lighting in this photo was provided by a flash on the camera used in conjunction with a hand-held reflector just to the right of the frame. Fill light should be transparent, never causing harsh shadows or blown-out highlights. Here, the fill light is well balanced with the ambient light and is very natural looking.

The sun acts as the main light in this shot. The boy who is in shadow still has a very good skin tone because the lighting on him is not all that different than on the other two. The other boys do have some specular highlights on their cheeks that the small boy does not, but the overall balance of lighting is very pleasing.

Camera: Canon EOS

Lens: 35-135mm zoom

Film: Ilford XP2, rated at E.I. 200

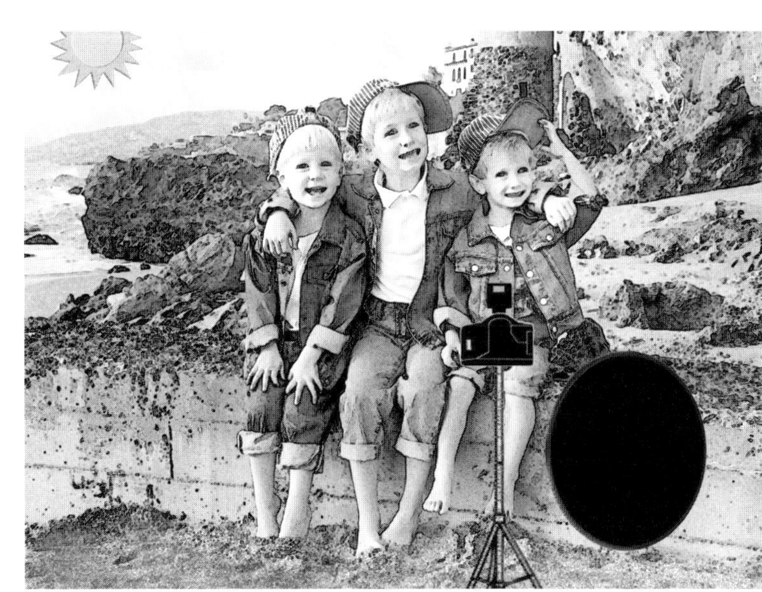

An on-camera flash and a reflector provide fill light for this portrait. The main light is the sun from camera left.

•Posing

It is nice to have calm and relaxed pictures, and not high energy ones all the time. This little lady is gazing out a window looking calm and very relaxed. For this image, the girl was posed on a wooden bench. We set this bench against several different wood fences for backgrounds. The differing textures of the fences make for interesting backgrounds and add some extra interest to the image.

"It is nice to have calm and relaxed pictures ..."

•Available Light

Again, this image was taken with all natural window light, which necessitated a long exposure. In this situation we used a fast lens (a 50mm f-1.8 lens wide open with the camera set on a tripod) to give us the needed depth of field. For this situation, we normally use a shutter speed of 1/60 second. However, if the subject is a little wild and bouncing around, under these exposure conditions she will be out of focus or blurry to due her movement. If your subject won't sit still, studio lights are preferable to natural light. If you still want to use natural light, consider a faster film (400 ASA is safe) and a smaller aperture. Kodak 3200ASA film is another possibility. It has a wonderful grainy look, but could be problematic if you want to make wall-size portraits. Decide what look you want and make the best decision to meet your client's needs.

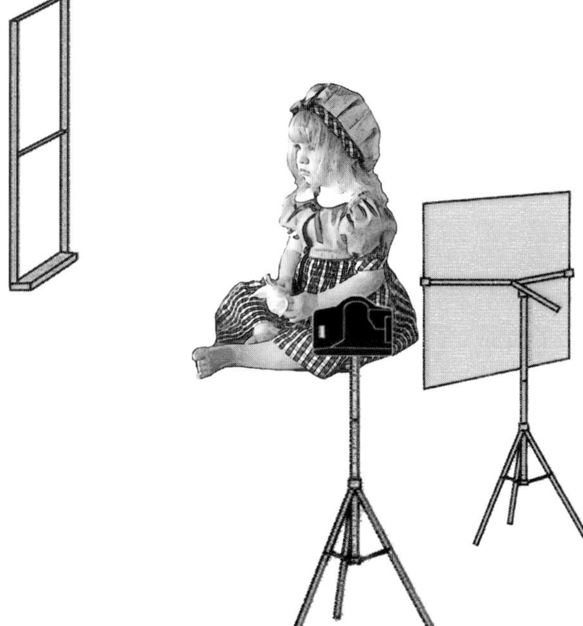

Camera: Canon EOS

Lens: 50mm, f-1.8

Film: Kodak TMX100, rated at E.I. 80

Natural window light illuminates the subject from the left of the camera. A large reflector panel was used to bounce back some of the light from the opposite side of the subject.

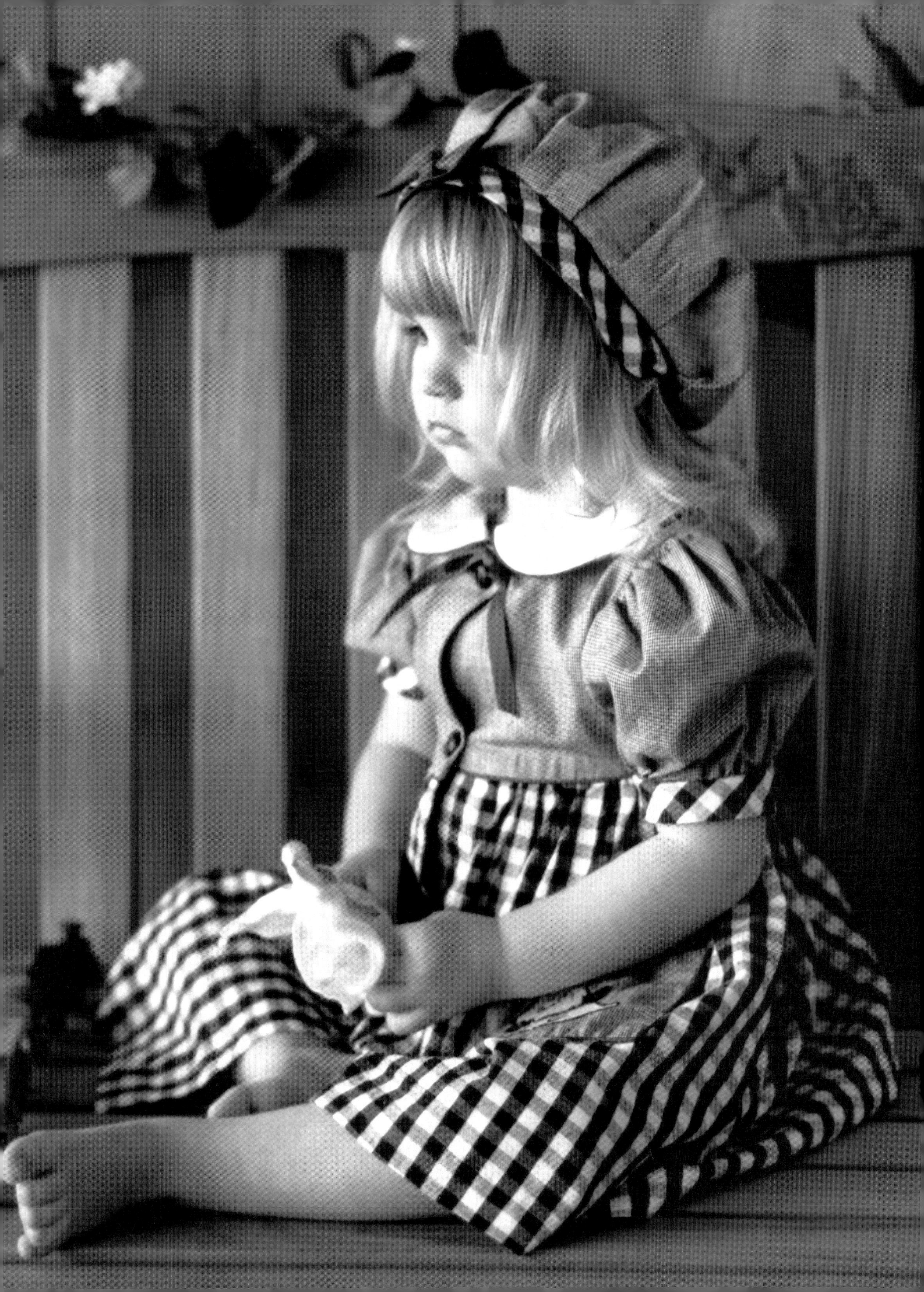

•Lighting with Reflectors

There was a lot of dappled sunlight filtering through the trees during this shot, so my assistant had to walk around with a reflector panel until he found a patch of sunshine and reflected it back into her face. We wanted to keep the back-lit rim light on her hair and arms (which was well defined against the dark background). When using a reflector, it's a good idea to search around till you find just the right angle. In this instance we decided to place the light-haired girl against the dramatic dark background of the tree. You can see the specular quality of light from the silver reflector in the highlights on her face.

"We wanted to keep the back lit rim-light ..."

•Processing Film

We process all our film because it gives us control over how the final image will look. We use a standard processing routine to develop all the film. We find it is more efficient to standardize the processing, then choose different films to achieve the lighting and contrast that we desire. We always carry different types of film in our camera bag, depending upon the lighting situation. The film used was on this shoot was Agfa APX 100. For our process, it yields a higher contrast than Kodak TMX 100 (although it would be possible to match the TMX to the APX with increased development).

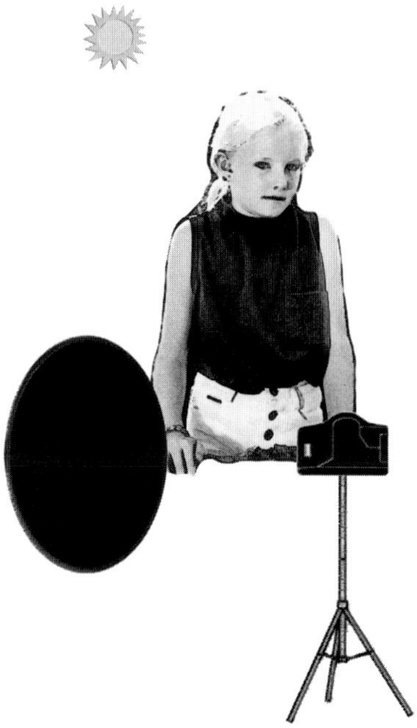

Camera: Canon EOS

Lens: 50mm, f-1.8

Film: Agfa APX 100

Sunlight was reflected back onto the subject's face to illuminate it amidst the patchy light in the shade of the tree. The sun at her back creates nice rim-lighting.

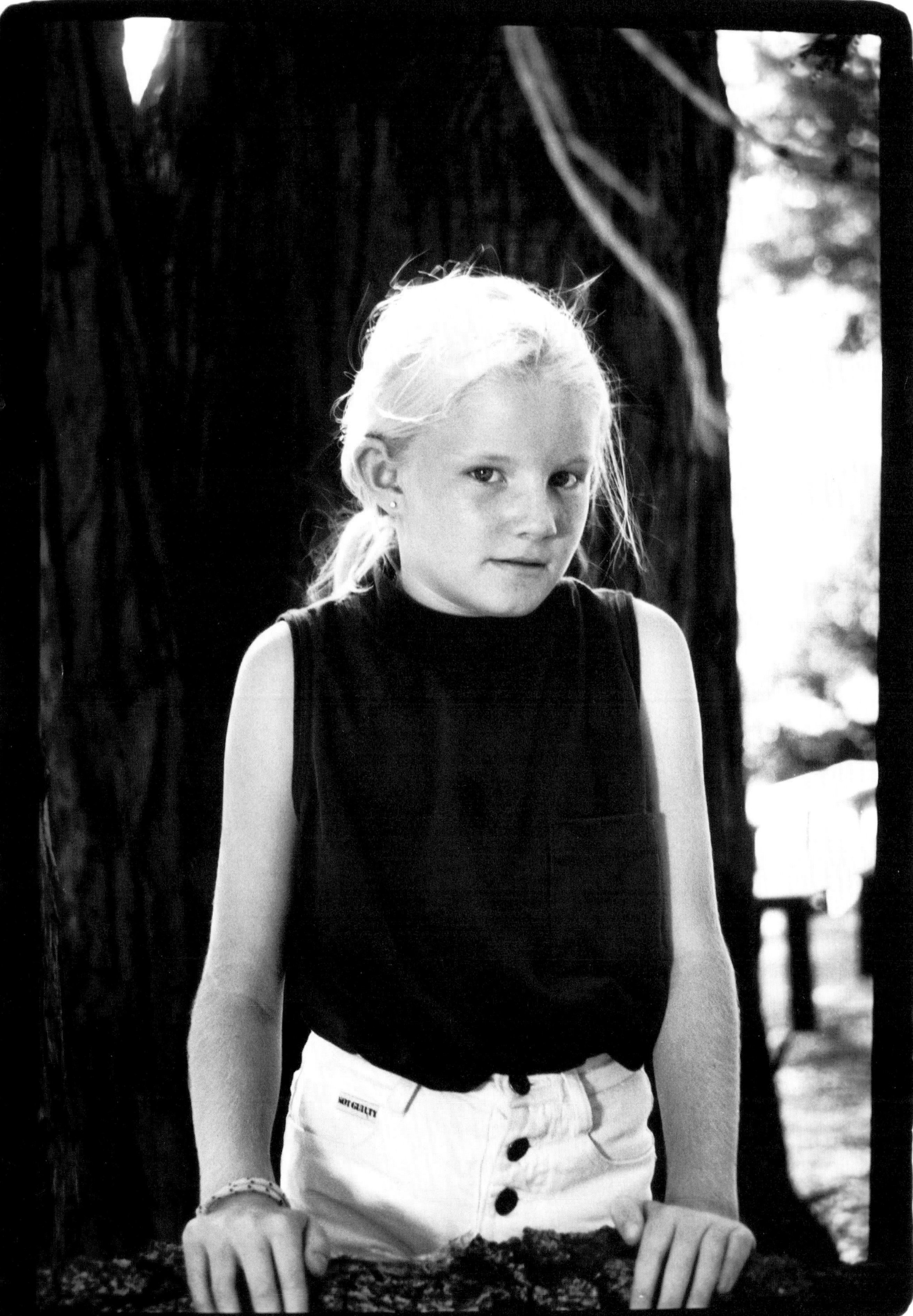

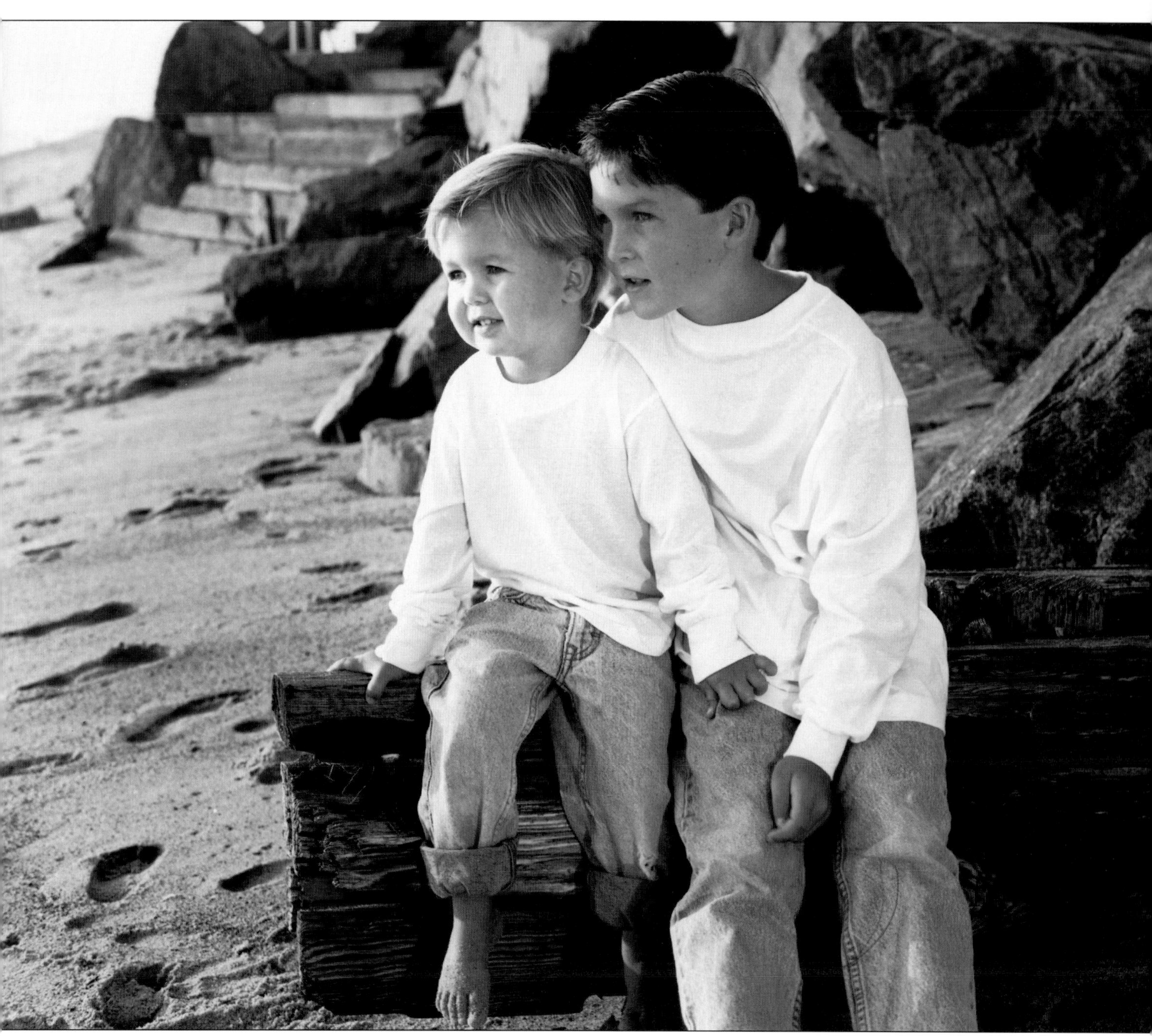

"It is an optimum time because of the exceptional light ..."

•Late Day Light

We shoot a lot of our portraits in the late afternoon. It is an optimum time because of the exceptional light available.

•Fill Flash

One of the conditions we encounter when shooting just before sunset is that the subjects are strongly back-lit. Overcoming this requires a stronger fill light than you can get from an ordinary on-camera flash unit. In this case it was necessary to use a Norman 400B flash. The Norman provides us with enough power to balance out the brightness of the sunlight.

As the sun nears the horizon and the ambient light becomes darker, you may be able to decrease the power setting on the flash or increase the distance between the strobe and the subjects. As the sun sets, we are generally able to turn off the flash and use an on-camera flash unit to fill in the shadows.

Camera: Pentax 645

Lens: 75mm leaf-shutter

Film: Kodak TMX100, rated at E.I. 80

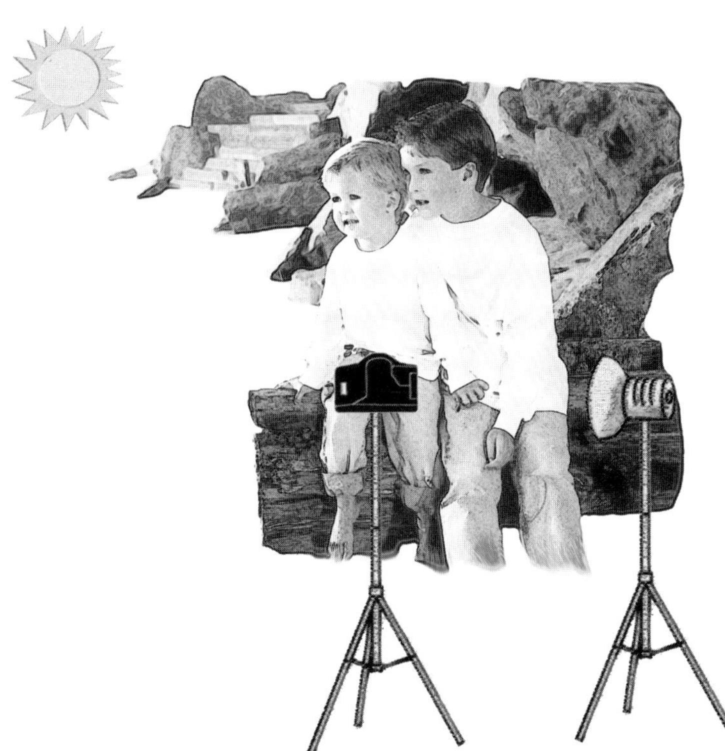

With the sun at a low angle, more fill light is often needed than can be provided by an on-camera flash. For this shot, a Norman 400B flash head was used for fill.

•Posing

This is a strong portrait of a young lady. Her serious looking little eyebrows and the fist placed squarely under her chin make a powerful statement. There is a definite Victorian look to the portrait that is emphasized by the clothing and the hat.

This was not a posed shot; it is how the girl decided to position herself. We went with it and continued to shoot.

•Hats

People don't wear hats nearly enough these days. Hats work very nicely to keep the hair in place if the wind is blowing. They also make the ordinary portrait a little more ornate, and nicely frame the subject's face.

•Composition

This photograph has some very nice leading lines that direct your look to the girl's face. The highlight on the rock on the left leads your eye right up to her face and eyes, as does the curved part of the rock in the background to the right.

"This is a strong portrait of a young lady."

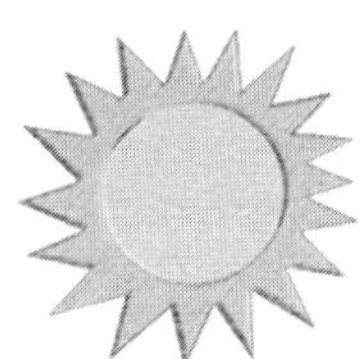

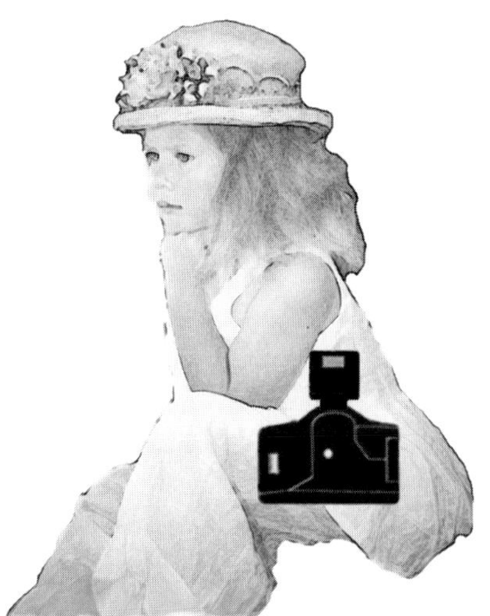

Camera: Pentax 645

Lens: 75mm

Film: Kodak TMX100, rated at E.I. 80

Fill light helps to illuminate the shadows in this portrait which is main-lit by the sunlight from camera left.

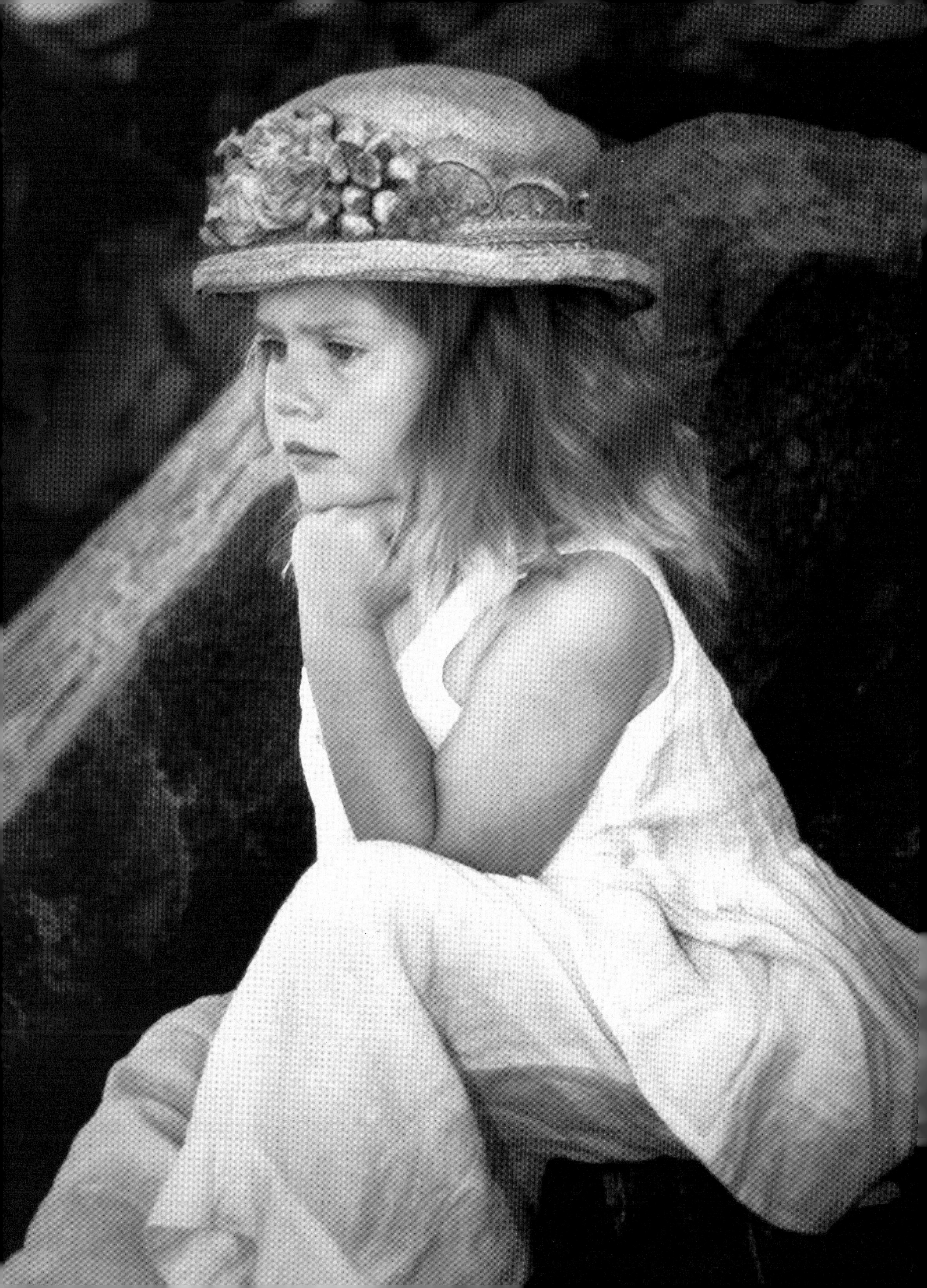

•Family Resemblance

Sometimes you just can't hide the fact the you're having a good time. This portrait of two sisters on a surfboard is a classic image of two kids having fun and just being themselves. The really wonderful thing about this shot is their poses. Their hands, feet and facial expressions are so much the same that there is no denying the family resemblance.

"... a classic image of two kids having fun and just being themselves."

•Lighting

We took this shot using no flash. We used only the back lighting to shoot, then printed the photo lighter than a full silhouette to reveal the expressions their faces and the details in their clothing.

•Documenting a Special Experience

It's always an honor to photograph someone's family. You get to meet exceptionally great families and the work is more like having fun. We have people tell us what a great experience it is to be photographed, and this is an important factor in creating great images. Clients treasure your images all the more when they are not just shots from a photo session, but memoirs of a lovely family experience.

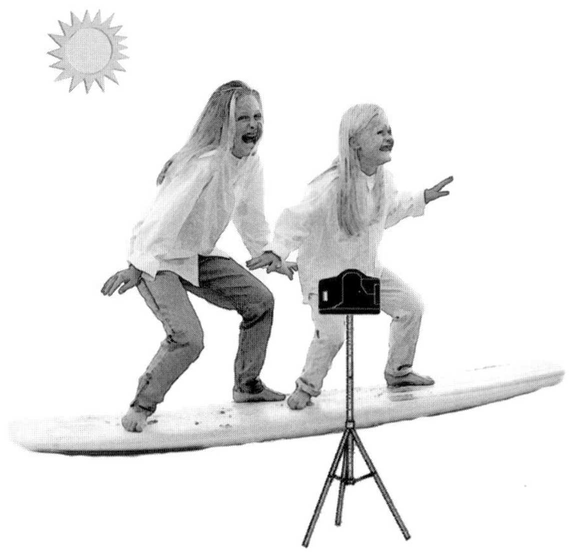

Camera: Canon EOS RT
Lens: 50mm, f-1.8
Film: Agfa APX 100, rated at E.I. 100

This portrait was shot using only existing light which came from behind the subjects. We then printed the image lighter than a full silhouette to show the girls' happy expressions.

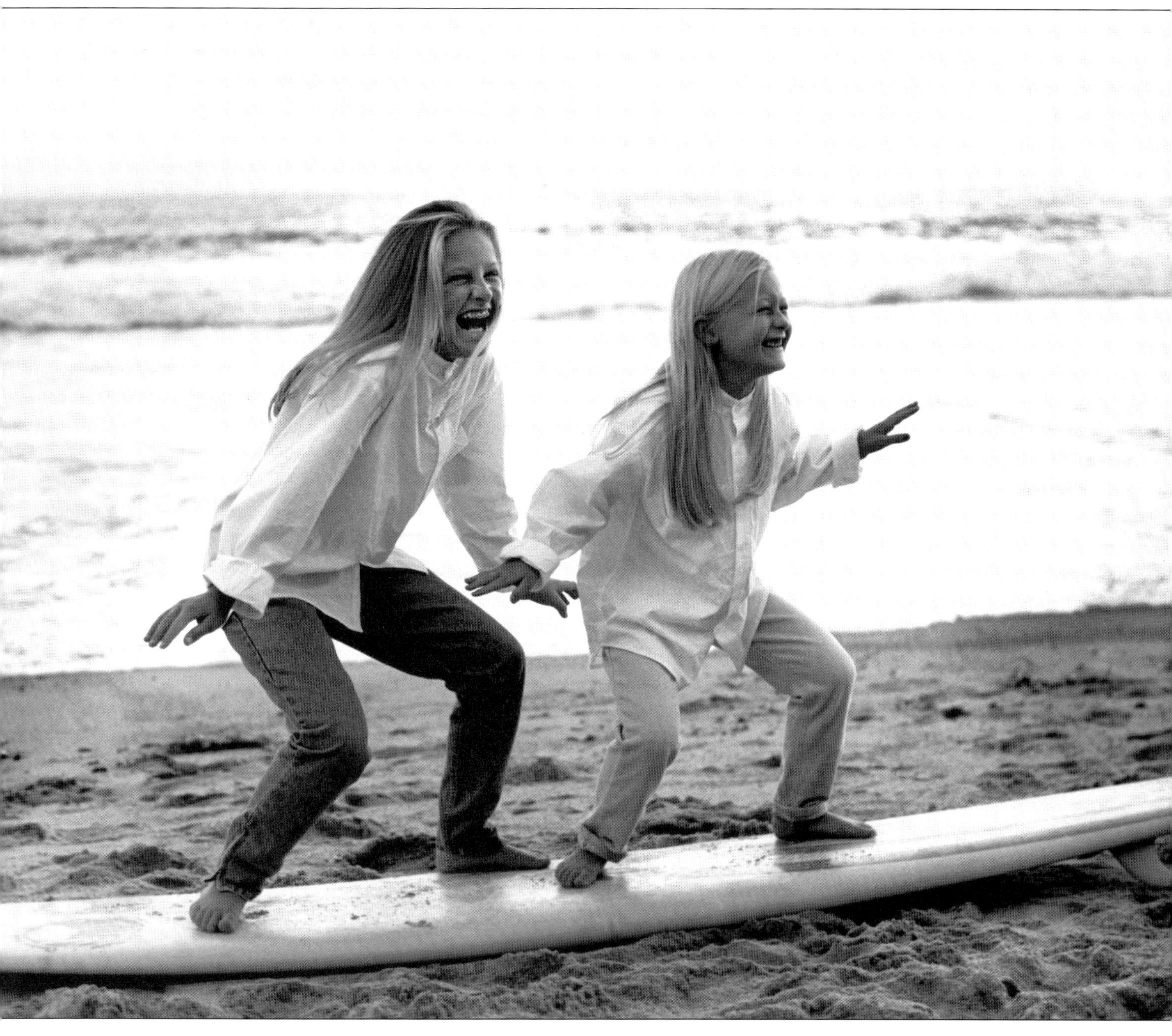

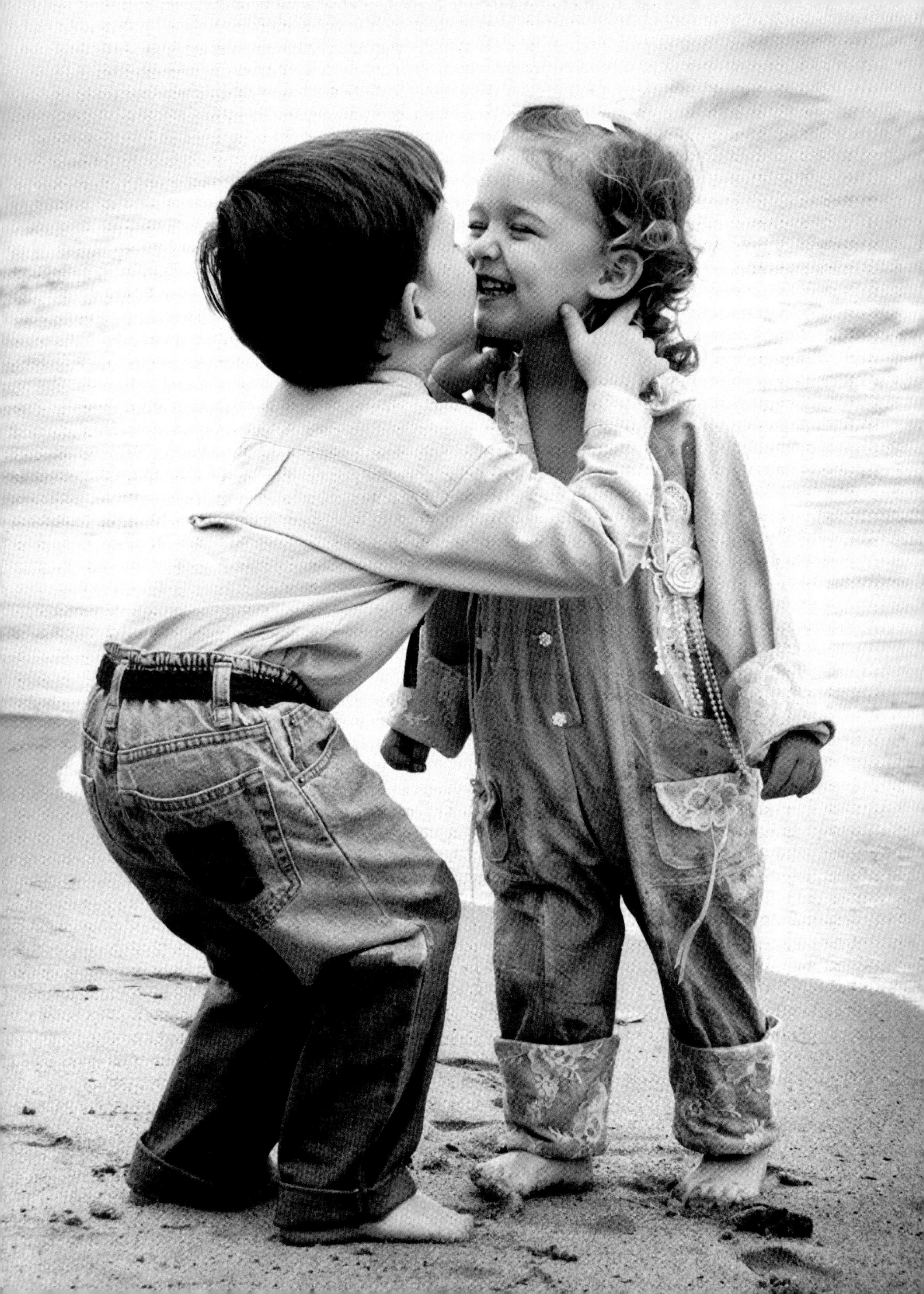

"... we gave them permission to have a good time ..."

•Permission to Get Dirty

Kids don't normally have permission to get all messy. We're always afraid that they're going to get their clothes all dirty, so it's normal for us to admonish them to try to keep clean and dry. During this photo shoot, we gave them permission to have a good time – to get their clothes all wet and to get sand on everything.They ran up and down the beach getting wet, getting covered in sand and burning up energy – you can almost feel the excitement.

•A Spontaneous Moment

The special thing about this picture is the expression of anticipation on the little sister's face. She is smiling with her eyes closed and giggling just waiting for her brother to kiss her. Her hands are tight and her toes are all crunched up.

Amid all the activity of getting wet and messy, they came up with this spontaneous little moment. You always have to be prepared for anything to happen or you'll miss the moment and it will be gone.

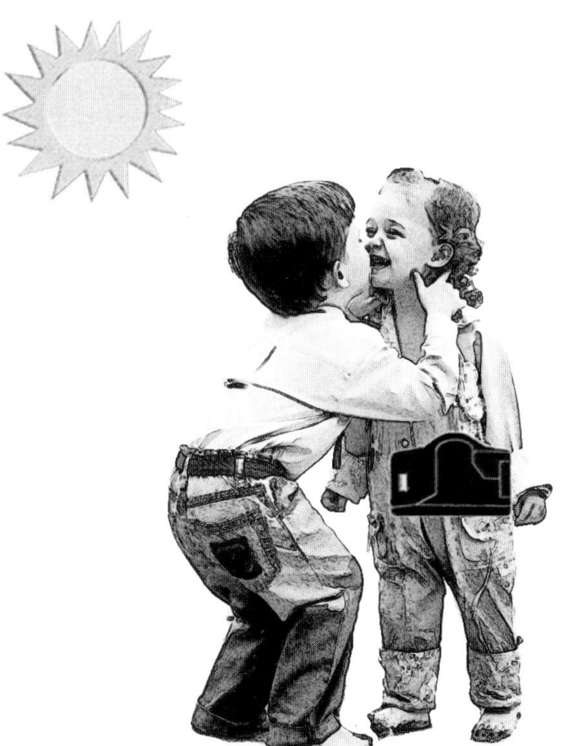

Camera: Canon EOS 630

Lens: 35-135mm zoom

Film: Ilford XP1, rated at E.I. 200

Natural light on a foggy morning was used for this portrait. The diffuse light is soft on the subjects and create very open shadows on them.

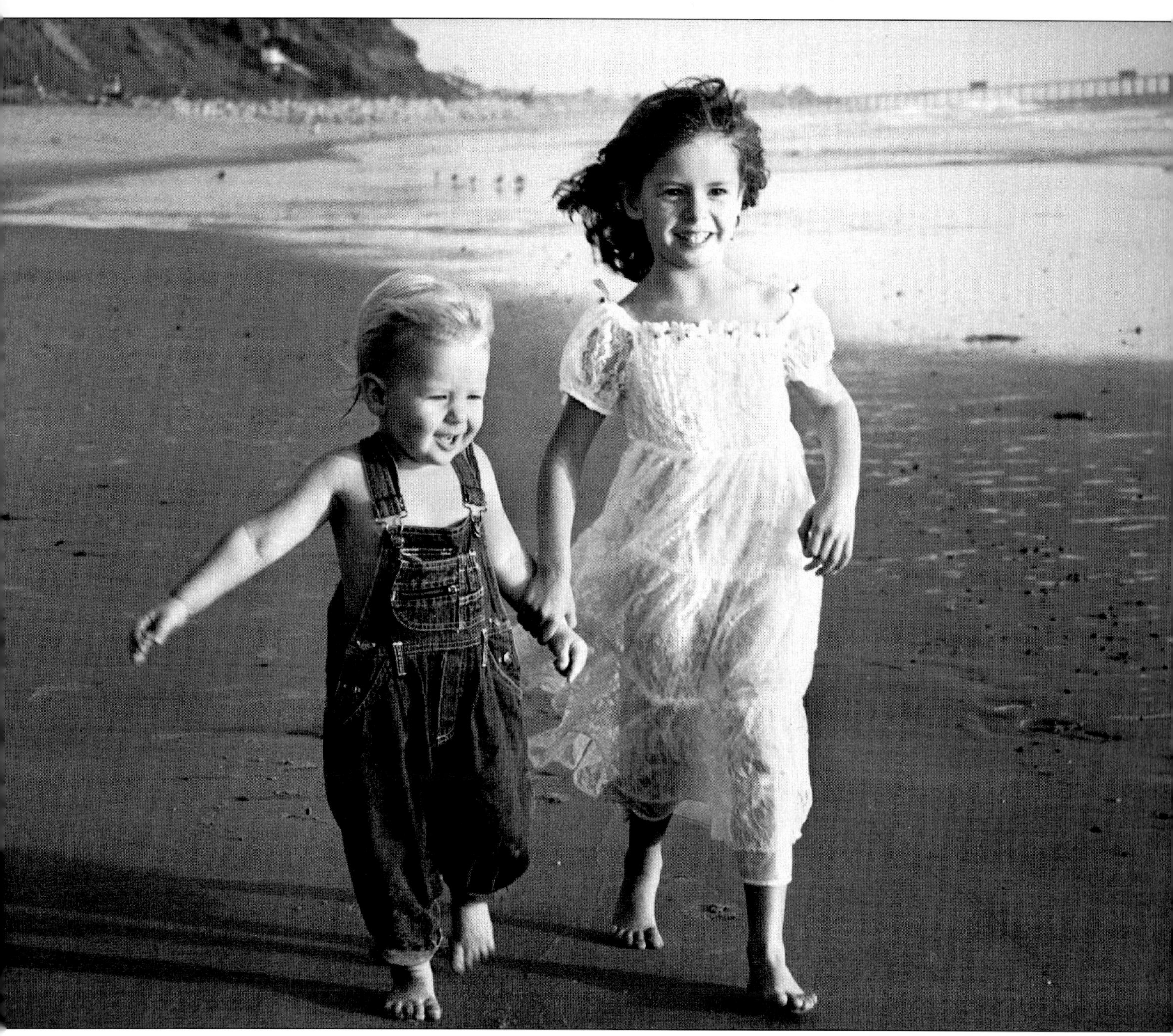

•Retakes

Here we have just two kids on a warm summer afternoon letting go of some energy and running down the beach. It could be a street or park or just about anywhere you let kids run around.

"... sometimes you just have to keep trying ..."

It sounds pretty easy doesn't it? Well sometimes you just have to keep trying until you're sure that you have the shot that the parents paid you to get. To get this one frame we shot a little over two rolls of film. We had to get just the right expressions on their faces. Their heads had to be looking up so they weren't staring at the ground. We had to get the feet right, and the arms right, and keep it all in focus by tracking them as they ran. We had to send them back and forth many times before everything clicked.

•Late Afternoon Light

This was shot at that magical time in the late afternoon when the beautiful long light envelopes everything with a wonderful golden glow. With the sun so low in the sky, the cross light gives exceptionally nice molding light to show off the full-length figures of these children.

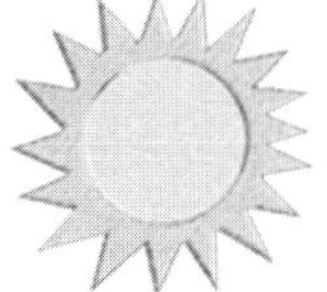

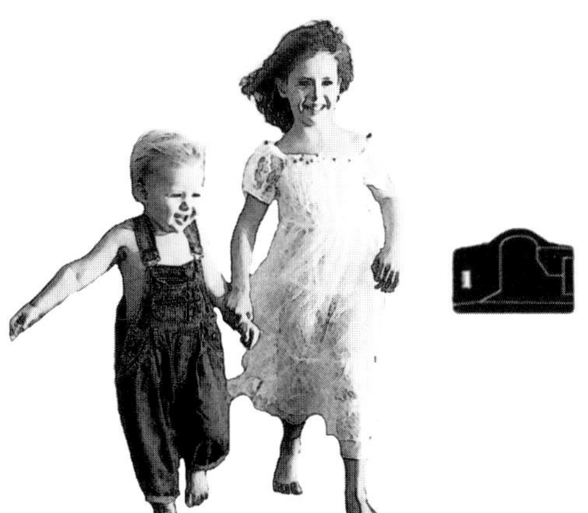

Camera: Canon EOS RT

Lens: 50mm, f-1.8

Film: Ilford XP2, rated at E.I. 200

The long light of late-afternoon sun was used to illuminate these two children on the beach. The directional quality of the light yields excellent texture and molding to show off the full-length figures of the pair.

• Borders

Sometimes we like to play around a little and experiment with different ways of doing things. With this print, we decided to print it with sloppy borders. We print some of our photographs this way because we can display the image showing the whole rough edge of the photograph all the way out to the sprocket holes. Alternately, we can cut a mat to show just a black border around the print when it is matted. This forms a thin black line between the print and the mat.

"Sometimes we like to play around a little ..."

• Cropping

One thing that is unavoidable when printing like this is that you must print the negative showing the full frame with no cropping. So whatever is in the frame is there on the print, and there is not much you can do about it.

• Lighting

This was shot about one half hour before sunset on a windy day. There is a special quality to the light when, on a cloudy day, the sun approaches the horizon and suddenly breaks through under the clouds. The light is much more directional and has a certain quality that is unlike light at any other time.

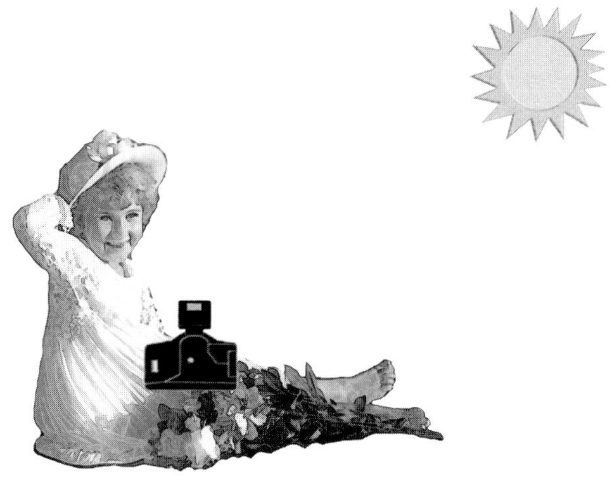

Camera: Canon EOS 630 with on-camera flash

Lens: 35-135mm Canon zoom

Film: Kodak TMX 100, rated at E.I. 80

With the sun as the main light to camera right, an on-camera flash was used as fill light to open up the shadows on the subject.

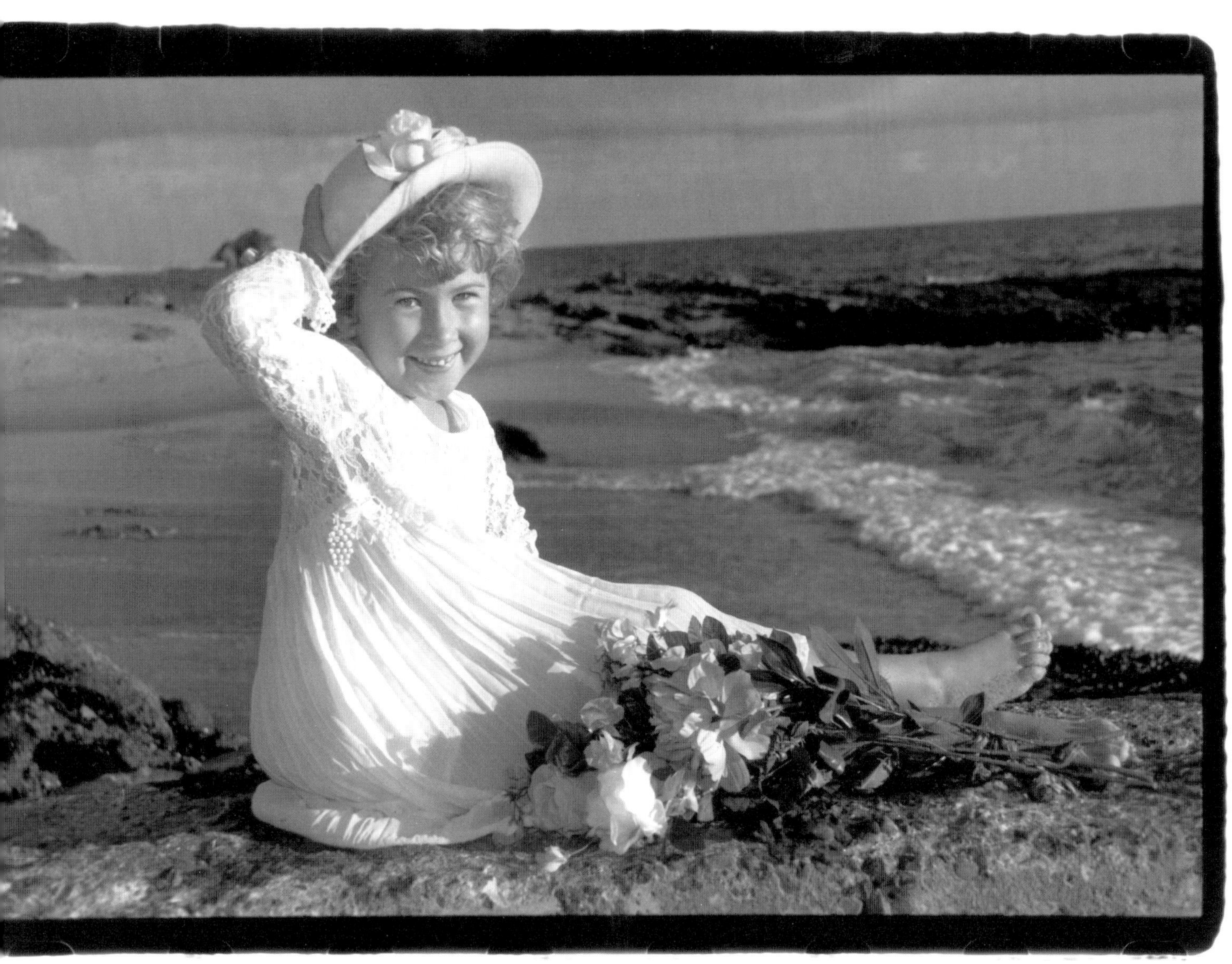

•Posing

The closeness of the brother to his sister and the clasping together of their little hands makes a very sweet picture. By placing the little sister up on an elevated surface you can create a very easy position for the older brother to snuggle into.

"... the clasping together of their little hands makes a very sweet picture."

•Clothing

The children's white shirts help to soften the tones of their skin and fill light near the camera position helps to fill in the shadows. There is a wonderful contrast between the harsh wood background and the softness of the children's skin.

•Lighting

The long afternoon light makes the light in the portrait so beautiful. It's a nice soft illumination without the blinding squinty light that you encounter earlier in the day when the sun is high above the horizon.

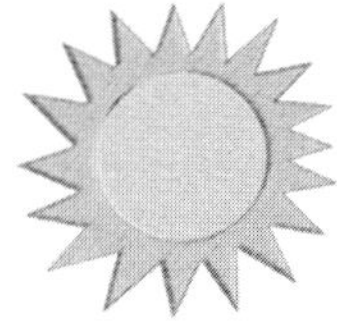

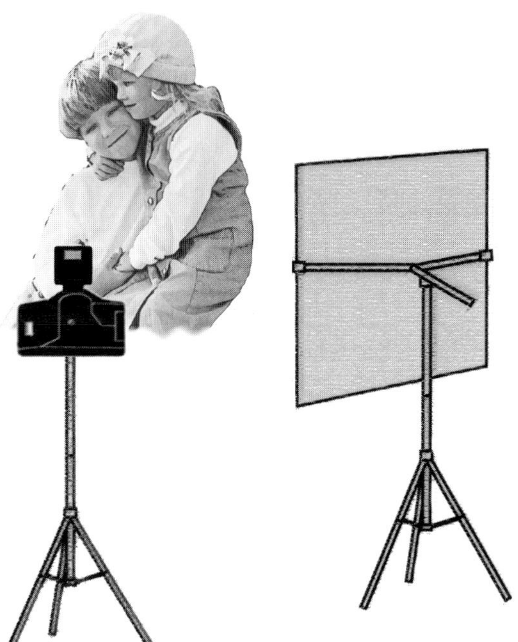

Camera: Pentax 645

Lens: 200mm

Film: Kodak TMX100, rated at E.I. 80

The children's white shirts bounce some light back onto their face to help soften the shadows created by the sunlight from camera left. A reflector and on-camera flash add extra light to open up these shadows.

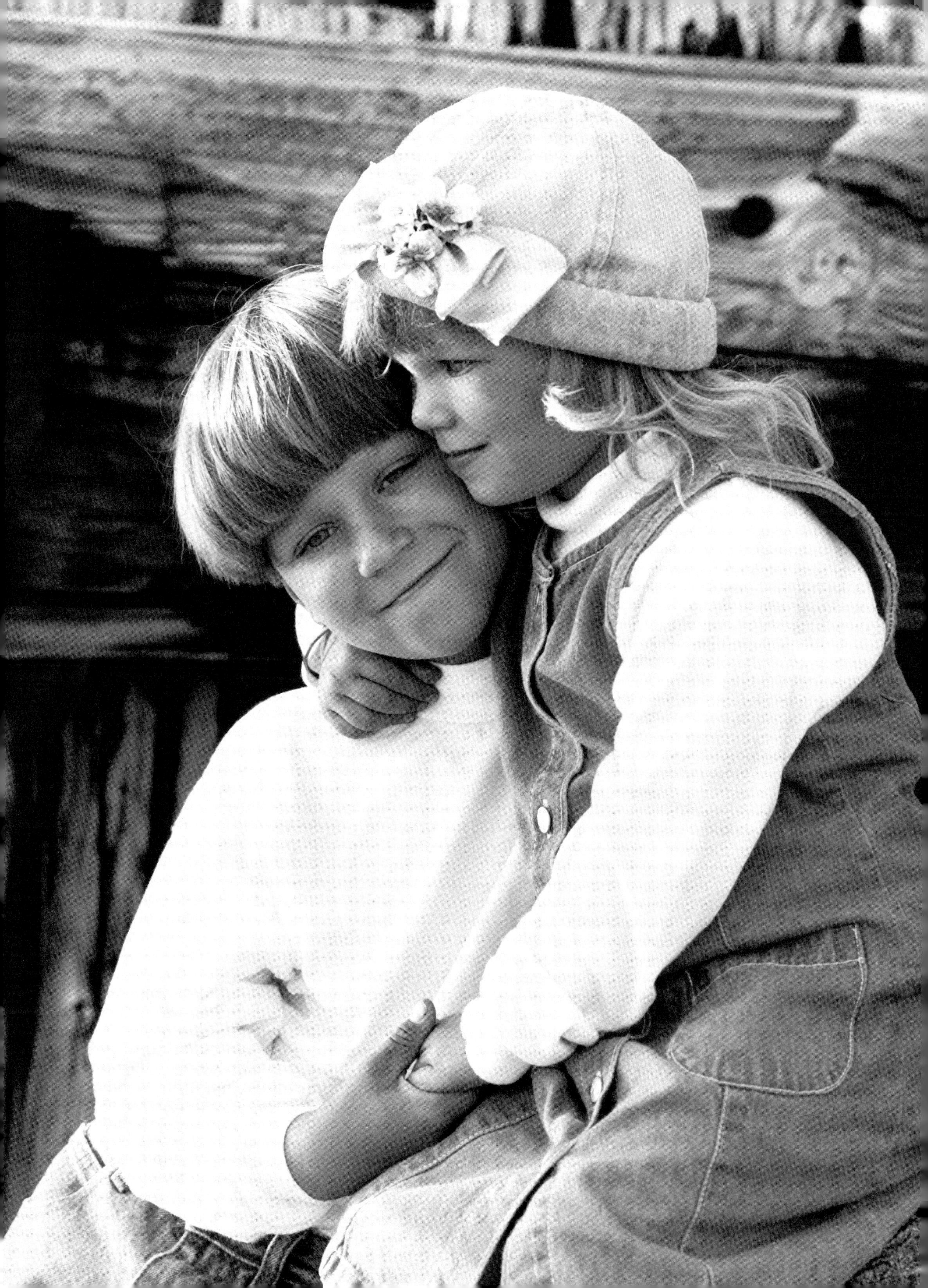

•Seasonal Flowers and Foliage

It's easy to get wonderful pictures with great natural backdrops. For about three weeks out of the year we have fields in California that bloom with blue lupine and other wildflowers. The fields are bountiful with beautiful flowers and long luscious grasses. During this span, we try to schedule shoots every single day so that our clients can benefit from these beautiful landscapes. We do advanced bookings for appointments months ahead of time just for those few weeks.

"... wonderful pictures with great natural backdrops."

•Outdoor Lighting

This photo portrays a boy giving a smooch to his little sister. It was taken after sunset when the sun is just over the horizon and the full open sky becomes a big diffuse light source.

Another great time of day we enjoy shooting in the fields is in the early morning when there is beautiful soft morning light. Admittedly, it's harder to get everyone up and ready to meet you at 7:00 a.m., but we're willing to go for it to get that remarkable portrait.

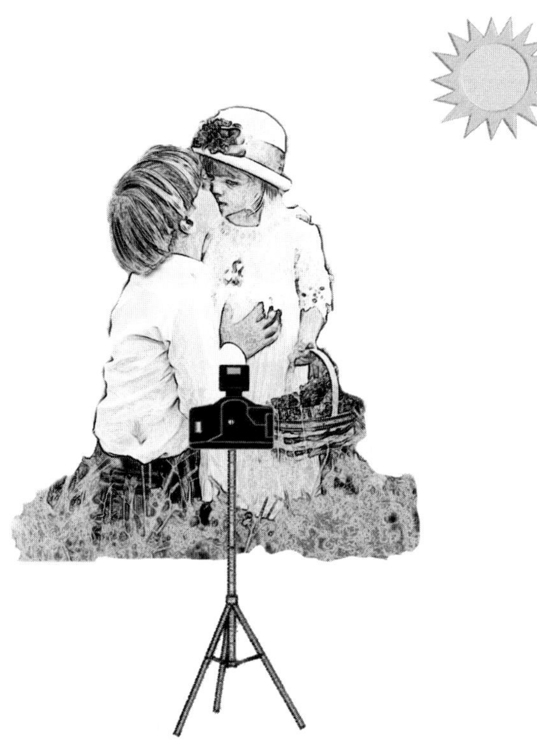

Camera: Pentax 645

Lens: 200mm

Film: Kodak TMX100

This portrait was shot just after sunset, when the full open sky becomes one big light source. A flash was used on the camera to provide fill light and open up the shadows.

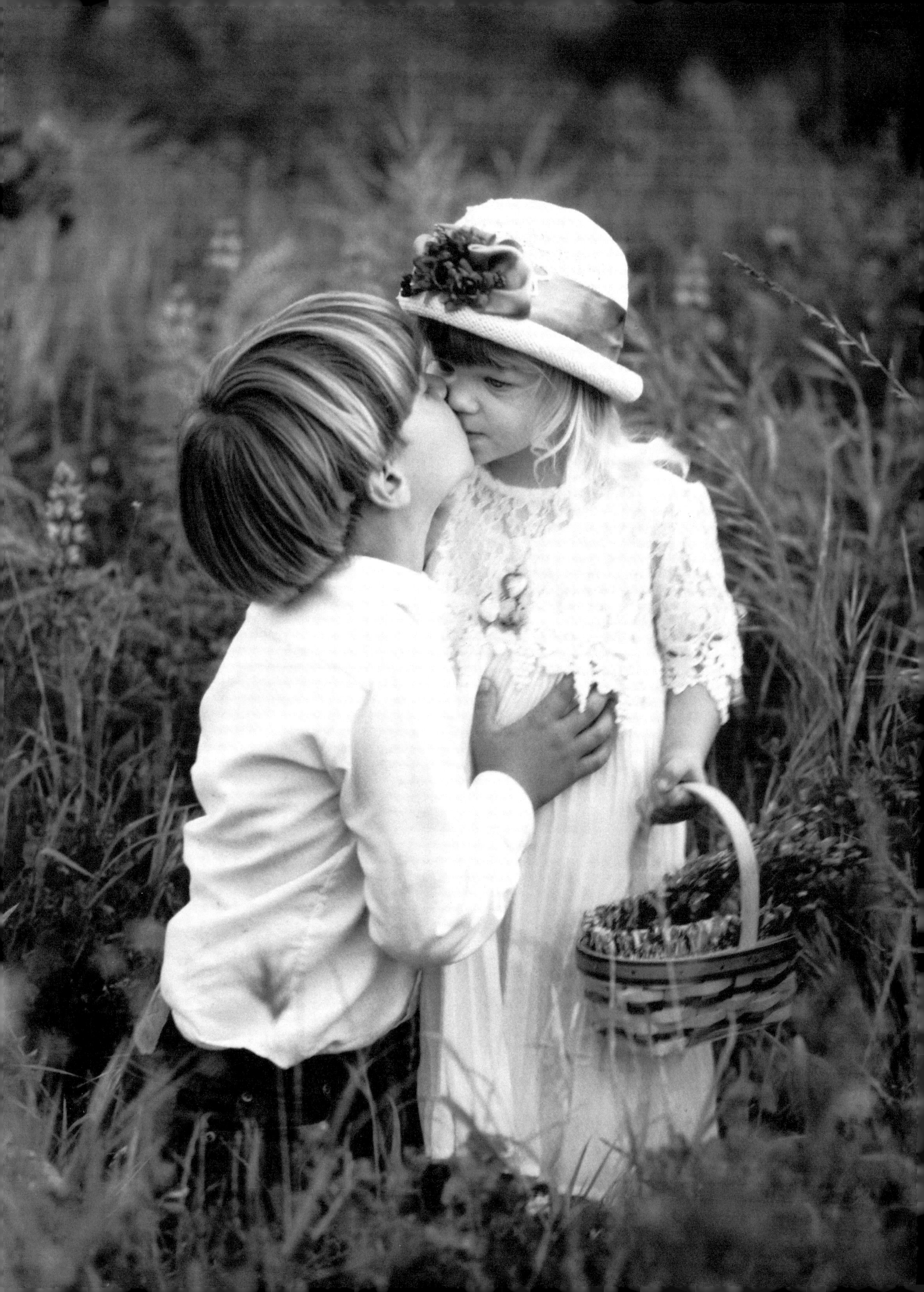

•Keeping Kids' Attention

These two little girls are ready to run wild. It often becomes necessary to do some dancing, play peek-a-boo, throw teddy bears into the air, tell some jokes, or have them tell you some jokes to get them to respond. This can get them in the right frame of mind to have their picture taken.

"These two little girls are ready to run wild."

•Bribes

We are huge believers in bribes. We usually have candy or goodies in the camera bag as treats for the kids. Ask the parents before mentioning anything about treats. Family rules or medical problems may prevent the children from having certain things. We don't provide any treats until the end of the shoot, no matter how much they beg, since this would defeat the purpose of having a bribe at all.

•Praise

You can always tell the kids what a great job they are doing. Even if they aren't doing the best job of cooperating, find something positive to say about how they are acting. It gives them a boost that may help you get more cooperation. Children can be negative or positive in order to get attention. It's in your best interest to evoke the positive aspect of their personality by acting positively toward them.

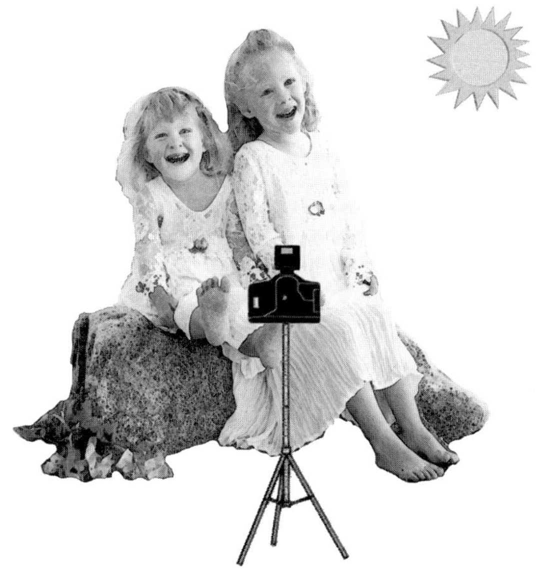

Camera: Canon EOS
Lens: 35-135mm zoom
Film: Kodak TMX100, rated at E.I. 80

The sunlight from camera right served as the main light for this portrait of two happy little girls on the beach. An on-camera flash was used to provide fill light to open up the shadows.

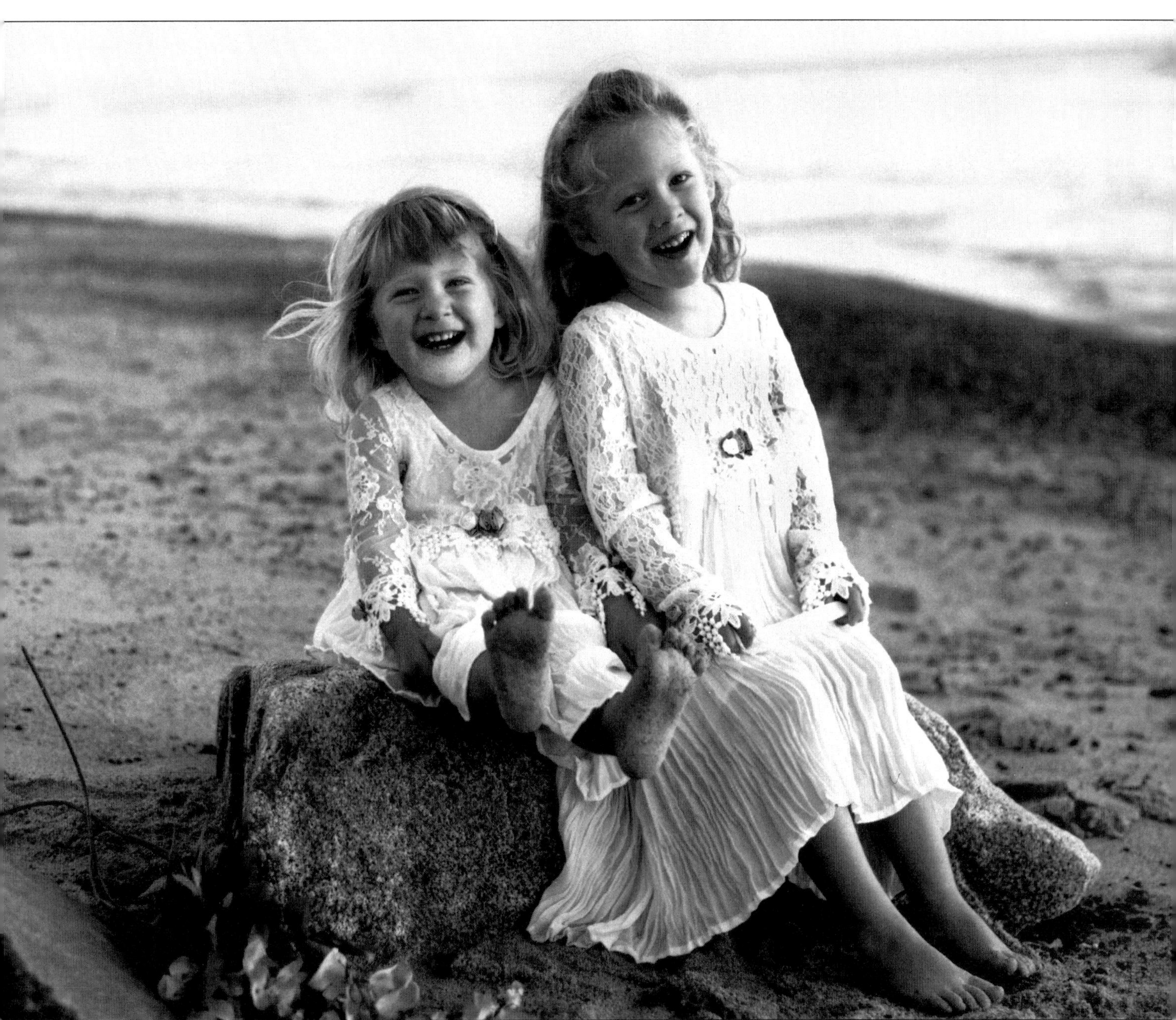

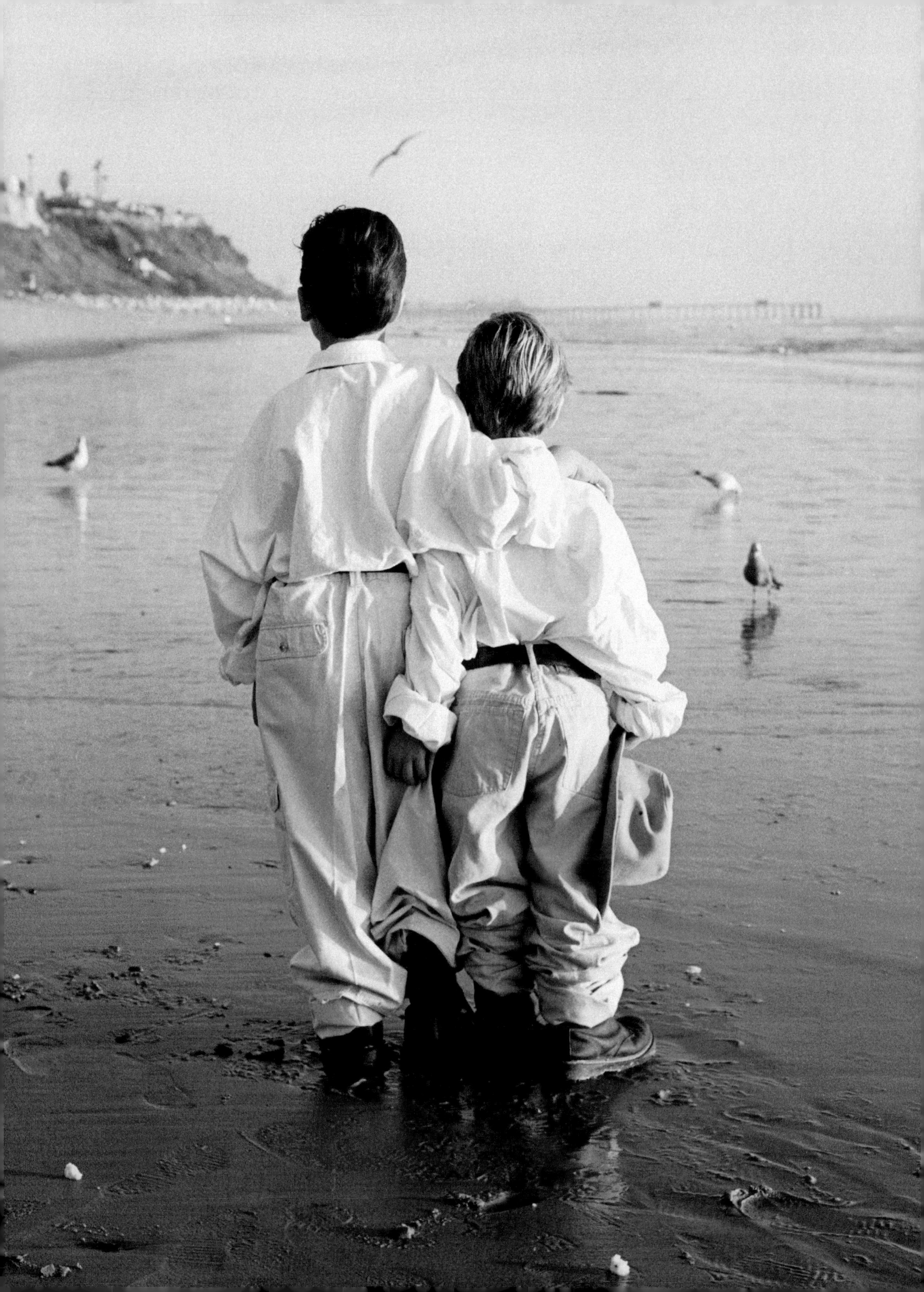

"We even had to leave coded messages ..."

•A Secret Shoot

It's always fun to be part of a surprises – and that is what made this photo shoot so much fun to do. Dad had to do some high-handed trickery to get the boys down to the beach without mom knowing about it. We even had to leave coded messages on the answering machine to set up the appointment.

•In Dad's Clothes

These were great little guys and real troopers throughout the whole event. We got them all dressed up in Dad's clothes and marched around on the beach and shot pictures for the afternoon.

•Late Day Light

This portrait was shot late in the afternoon. It was just before sunset and we used no artificial light – just the sun and the sky.

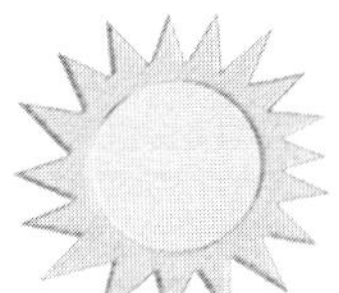

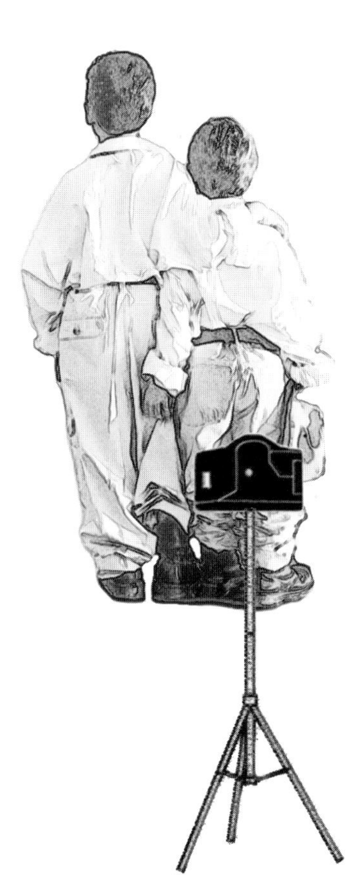

Camera: Canon EOS 630

Lens: 50mm, f-1.8

Film: Kodak TMX100, rated at E.I. 80

Late afternoon sun from camera right provided all the illumination that was needed to capture this sweet portrait of two little boys on the beach in their dad's clothes.

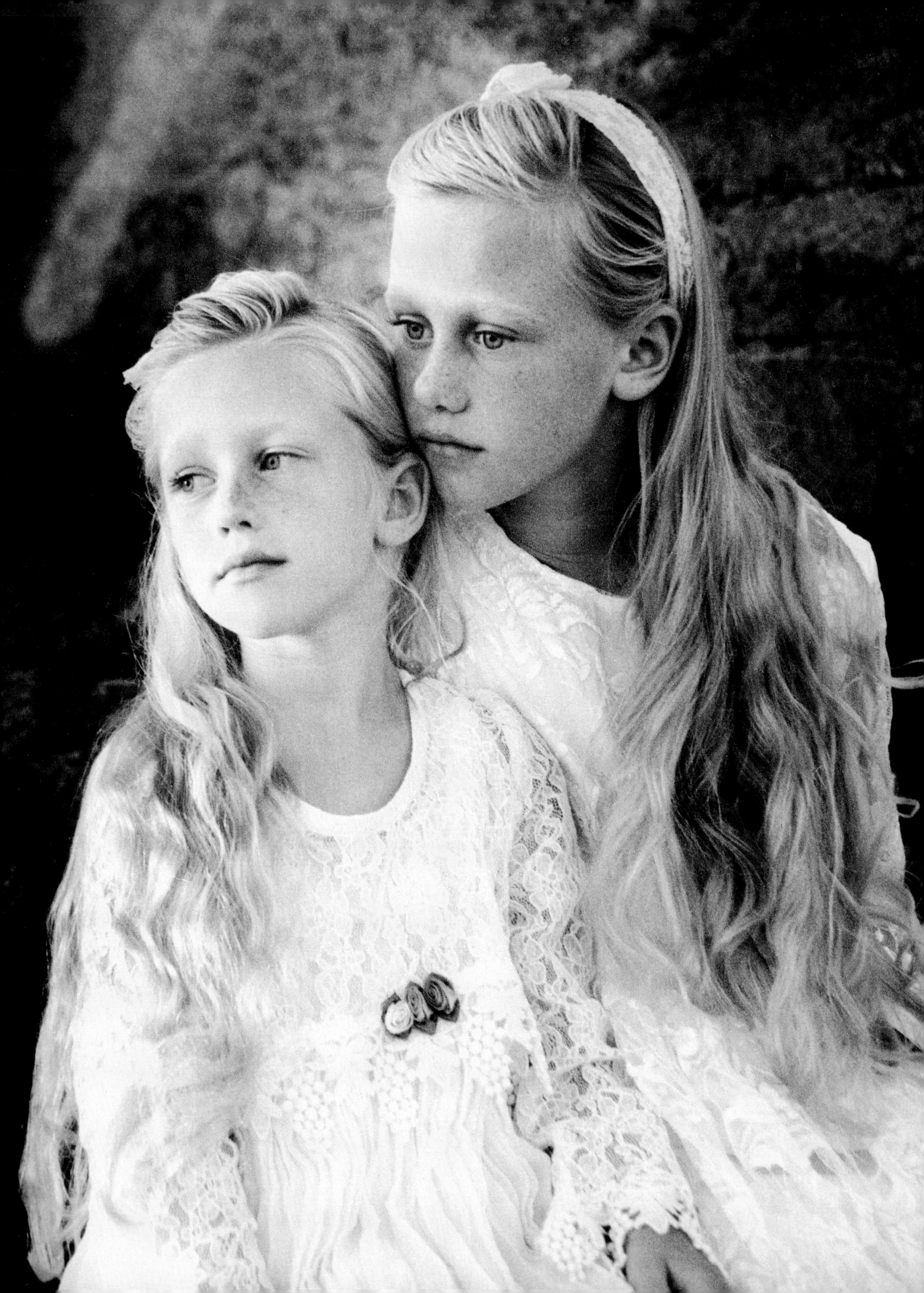

•Challenges and Surprises

We never know what we will get from a photo session. We always cover all the shots that are needed or wanted by the clients, but we also try to get that something extra that makes it fun and challenging.

"Where this photo came from is still a mystery ..."

During this shoot, we were having a good time and were near the end of the session. The girls were tired and were ready to go home. They were pushing and were all done being nice to each other. We had about five more shots to finish the sitting. Where this photo came from is still a mystery – the shots before it were terrible, and the shots following it were also bad. This lone shot is one of my all time favorite portraits.

As their mom and I looked at the proofs, we were stunned. Where did this come from? These girls are very beautiful, but the portraits caught so much more. The look in the girls eyes is so powerful and serene. I am always amazed how two or three frames shot within two seconds of each other have completely different looks.

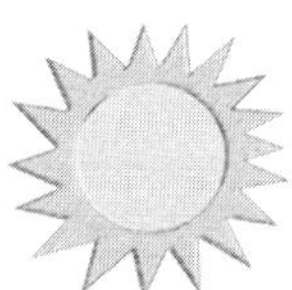

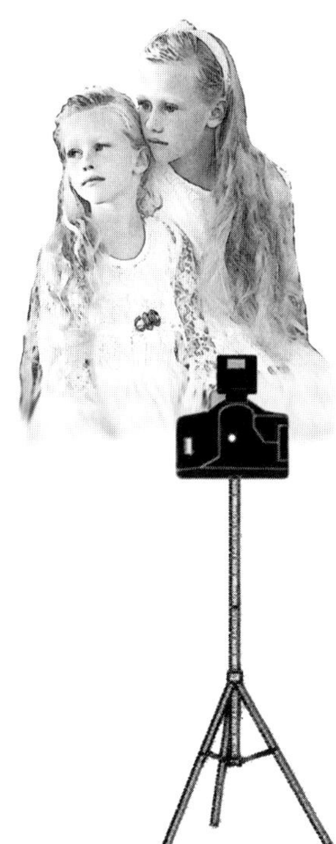

Camera: Canon EOS

Lens: 35-135mm zoom

Film: Ilford XP2, rated at E.I. 200

Natural sunlight from left of the camera served as the main light source for this portrait. An on-camera flash provided fill light to open up the shadows.

"That's what boys are all about at this age."

•Lots of Props

This boy wanted to have all his sports equipment with him in his photo. So he brought all of it – and we do mean *all* of it – with him to the session. That's what boys are all about at this age.

•Posing

The expression that he came up with for this photo was all him. There was no direction given. It wasn't contrived, it was just a matter of having a conversation with him and documenting his reactions. He was a very animated and fun kid to be around.

•Capturing Personality

The job of the photographer is to try to capture that unique personality, even though the subject is in the foreign (and often intimidating) environment of a photo studio. In this instance, it was a matter of the boy having all his things around him. That made it more comfortable for him so that he could be more relaxed.

Camera: Canon EOS 630

Lens: 35-135mm zoom

Film: Ilford XP2, rated at E.I. 200

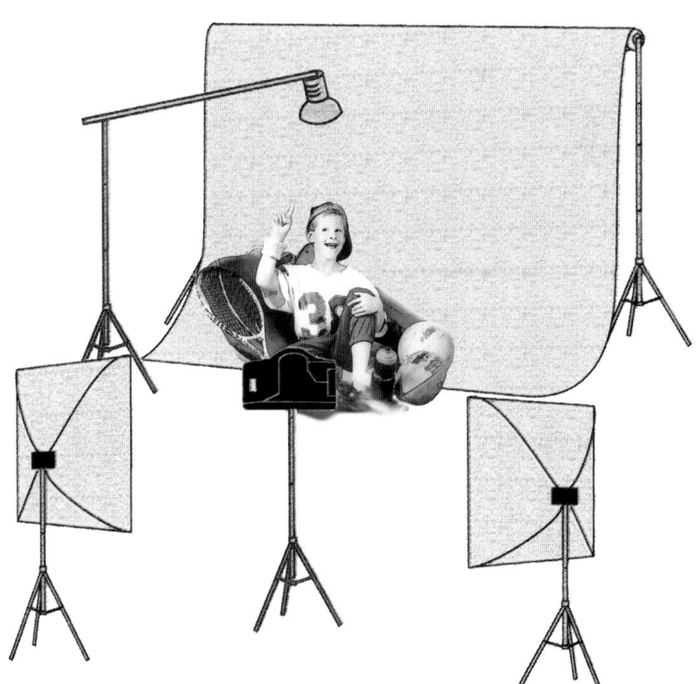

The main light for this shot comes from a softbox placed to the left of the camera. Another softbox is used at half-power from the right side of the camera to provide fill light. A hair light was added above the subject on a boom.

•Getting a Response

Every time we go out on a shoot we try to evoke a response from our kids so we'll have something interesting to photograph. It's a way to have some fun with a group of people, and makes the shoot more than just a photo session but an experience that you record.

"... we tickled their little feet and joked around with them."

This is one of those pictures that conveys the sense of pure joy of childhood. These kids are having a great time. Capturing it required being in the right place at the right time and being ready for anything. We got this reaction when we tickled their little feet and joked around with them. The only posing instruction we gave to them was to keep their heads together.

•Heads Together, Chins Down

When people look at the camera they usually have a tendency to lift their head up. So the mantra on my photo sessions is lower your chin and keep your heads together. I think it's much more intimate when heads are touching or close together.

•Lighting

This portrait was shot on a very gray and overcast day using natural skylight on a foggy morning.The light was quite diffuse so it wasn't necessary to have any fill light or reflector.

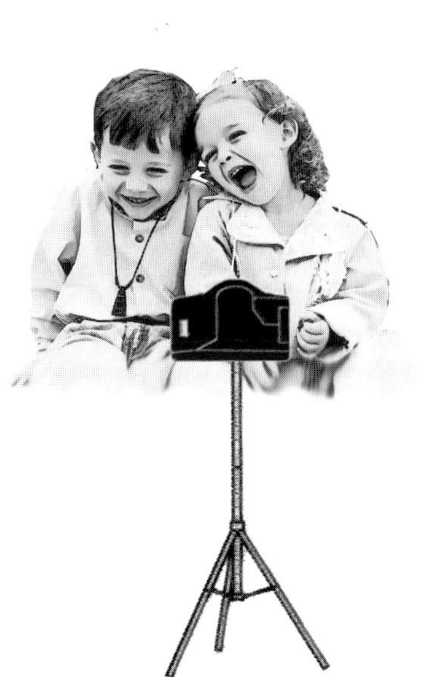

Camera: Canon EOS 630

Lens: 35-135mm zoom

Film: Ilford XP1, rated at E.I. 200

The diffuse light on this foggy morning made it unnecessary to use any fill light to create this soft, flattering portrait.

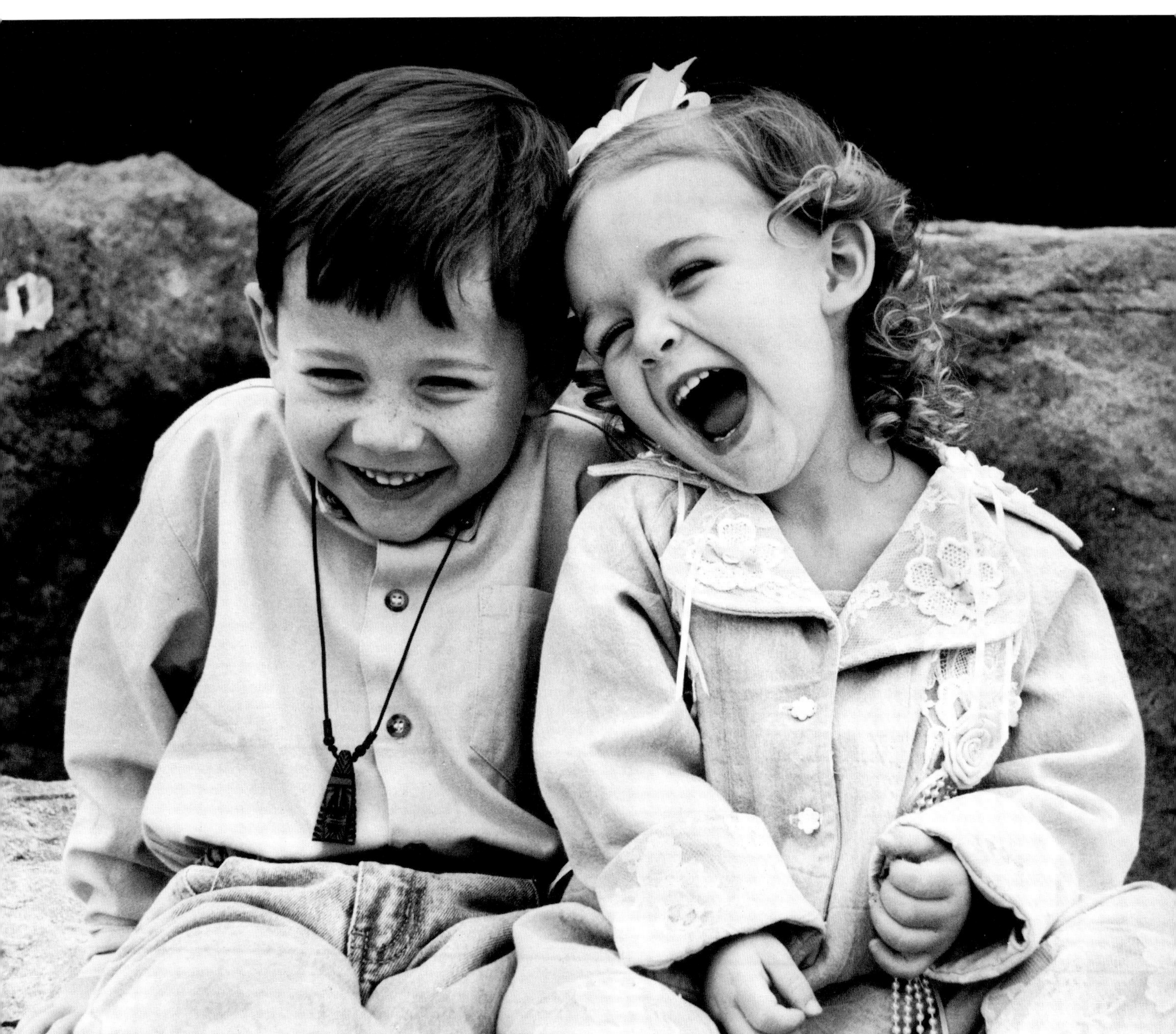

•Using Your Neighborhood

No matter what your neighborhood looks like, it just takes a little footwork to find some unique locations where you can shoot. It may be just an old fence with some weeds growing near it or perhaps some overhanging branches in a local park. Search out little doorways or gates, backyards, neighboring fields, and interesting building facades. Anywhere you can fit a couple of kids can make a unique backdrop for a great photograph. If your location is on private property, always ask for permission to shoot there. We don't usually get any hassle, but it's always necessary to ask.

"... it just takes a little footwork to find some unique locations ..."

This photograph was shot at a small local pony farm. It is just an old rusty antique bathtub that they use for watering the animals. The tub has a very country rustic look that complements the clothes in which the child is dressed. This has always been the picture on the last page in my portfolio.

•Lighting

The technique is very simple: on-camera flash with natural light coming in from the left causing a delicate highlights on the child's hair.

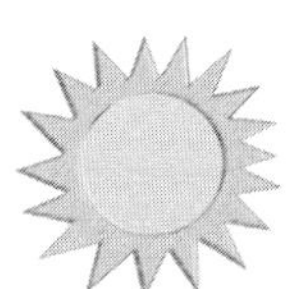

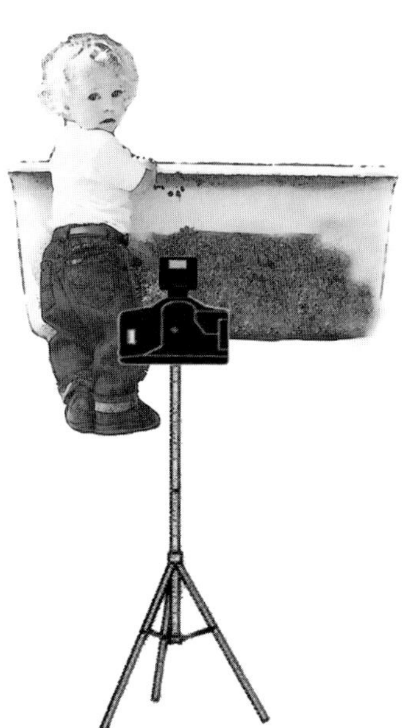

Camera: Canon FTB with
Vivitar 385 flash
Lens: 50mm, f-1.8
Film: Ilford XP2, rated at E.I. 200

An on-camera flash provides fill light, while the natural light from camera left causes highlights in the child's hair.

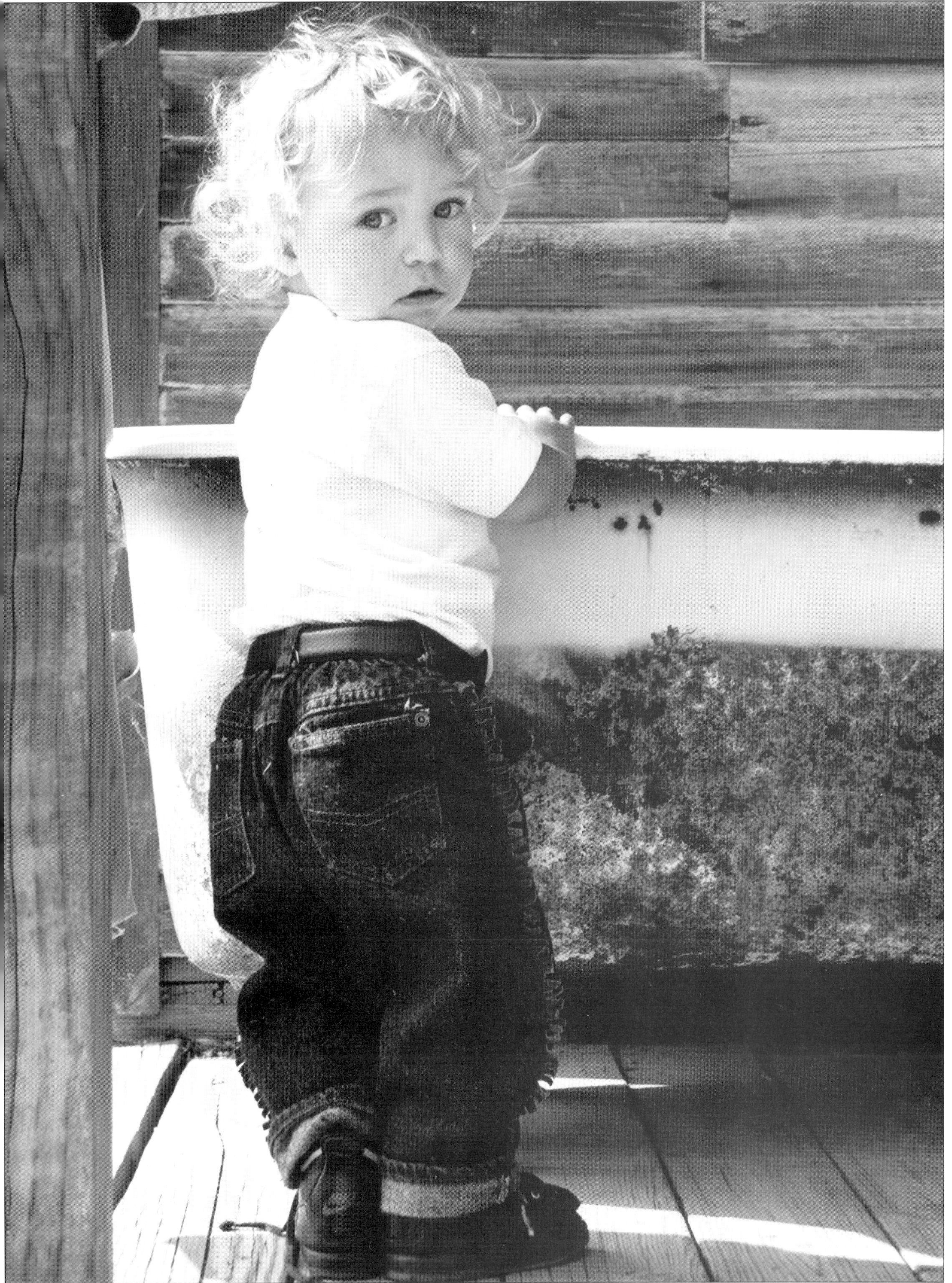

•Composition

In a photo you have people stuck in a rectangular frame. The borders of the photograph define the frame in which you see them. It's important in this type of picture to give the subjects somewhere to look. We put the subjects off center with more area in the frame in front of them than behind them to create this space. It makes them look less cramped and allows for an idea of movement.

"It's important ... to give the subjects someplace to look."

•Light

Normally, we use shadow to shape and mold the portrait image, but it is just the opposite in this photo. Here, we are using the specular quality of direct sunlight to shape the subjects' faces. The bright, specular sunlight outlines the older boy in the front and details the shape of his body. The highlights make the ripped knees of his jeans stand out. The sunlight shining on the little brother's face outlines his wonderful smile.

Camera: Canon EOS

Lens: 35-135mm zoom

Film: Kodak TMX 100, rated at E.I. 80

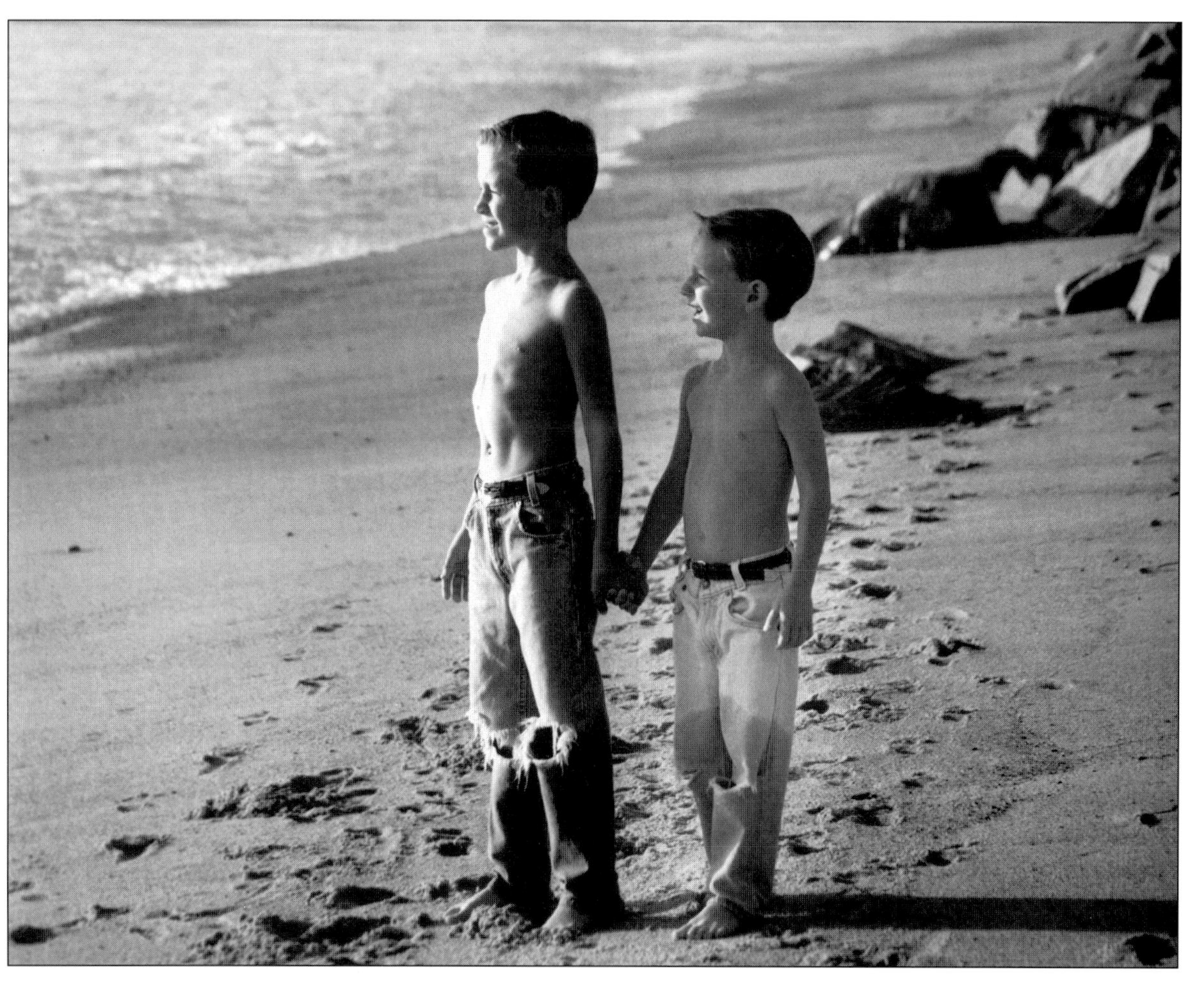

Kids and Hobbies

"The job of the photographer is to try to capture that unique personality, even through the subject is in the foreign (and often intimidating) environment of a photo studio."

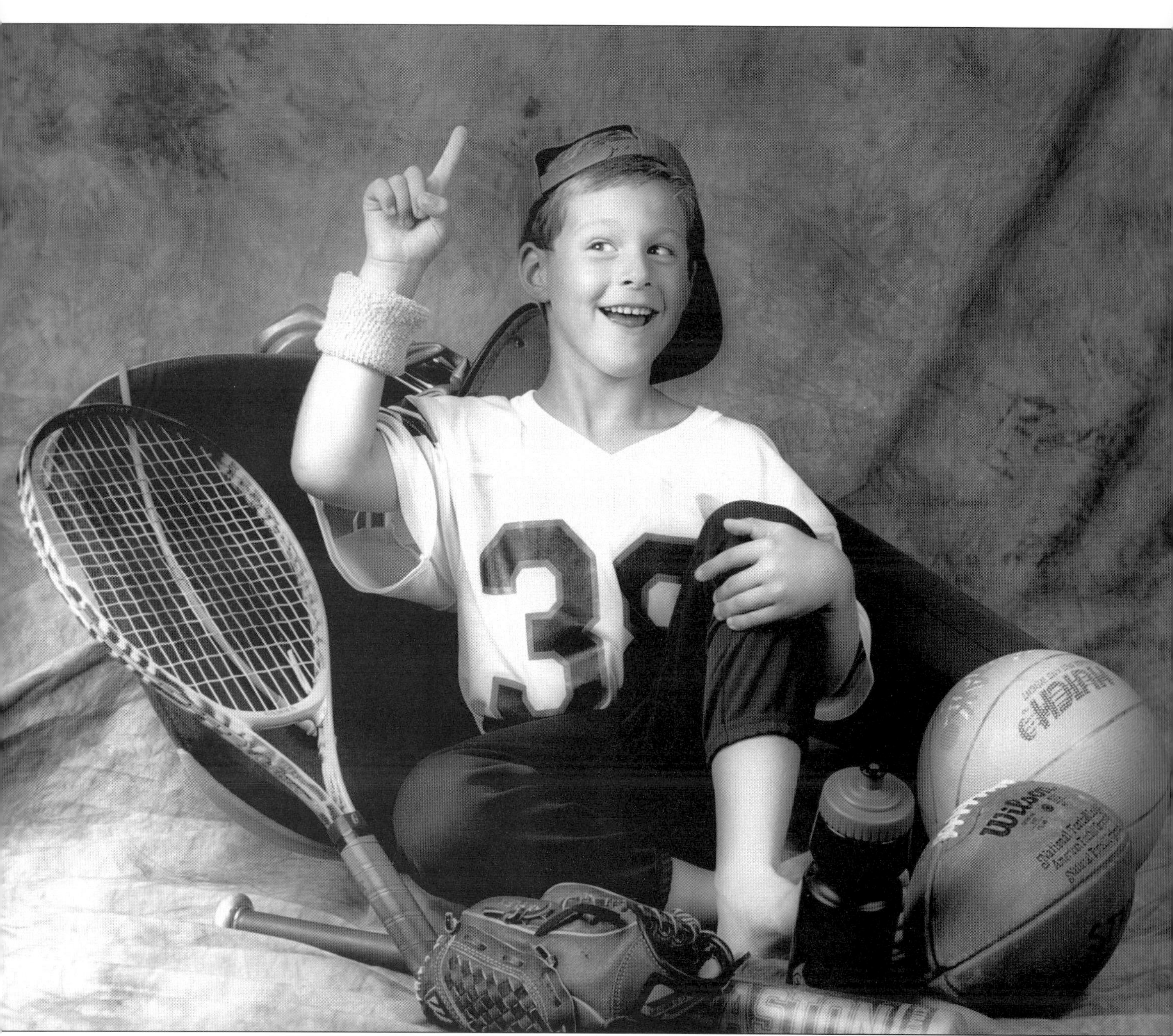
Wilson
ASTON

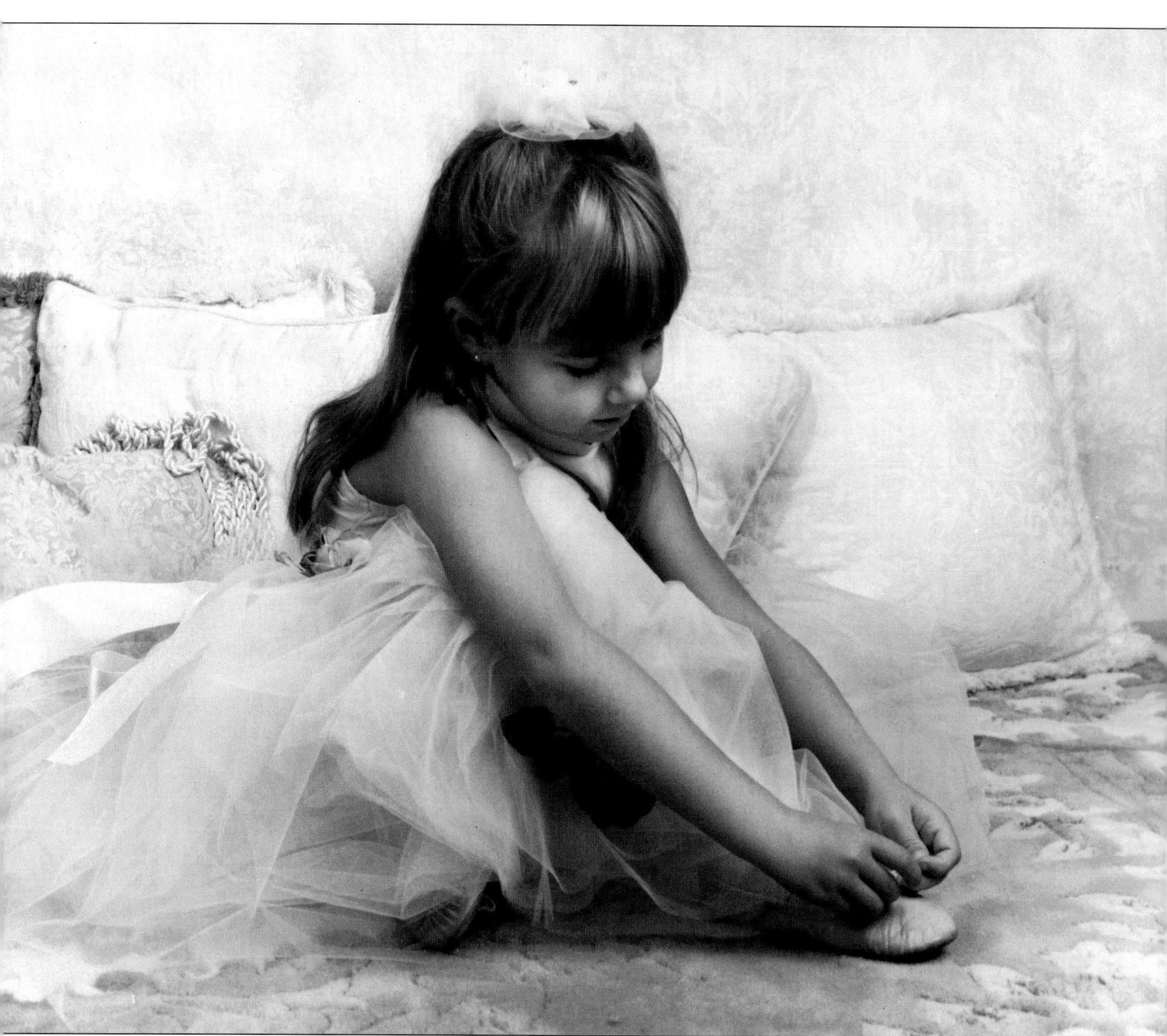

"Finally they bring a prized bull into the house ..."

•A Telling Story

We have a children's book about a photographer who is trying to take a picture of a farmer and his wife. The farmer and his wife keep going to get things they want included in the picture. Finally they bring a prized bull into the house and the whole photo session ends in disaster. Each time they go and get another thing the photographer's little assistant chimes in with,"Simple pictures are best."

•A Simple Pose

This photograph is really a very natural, and simple pose: a little dancer tying her ballet slippers. It's reminiscent of those Degas dancer paintings we've all seen. The pose captures the essence of a quiet moment before the dance. It's what makes this picture seem so serene.

•Composition

The composition of the photograph is based on the horizontal lines that go from the girl's hands tying her shoe, up the arms to her face and back down to the shoes. Your eye naturally follows these lines and leads you to look at her face and then down to her hands tying the dancing shoes.

Camera: Pentax 645
Lens: 75mm leaf-shutter
Film: Kodak TMX100 rated at E.I. 80

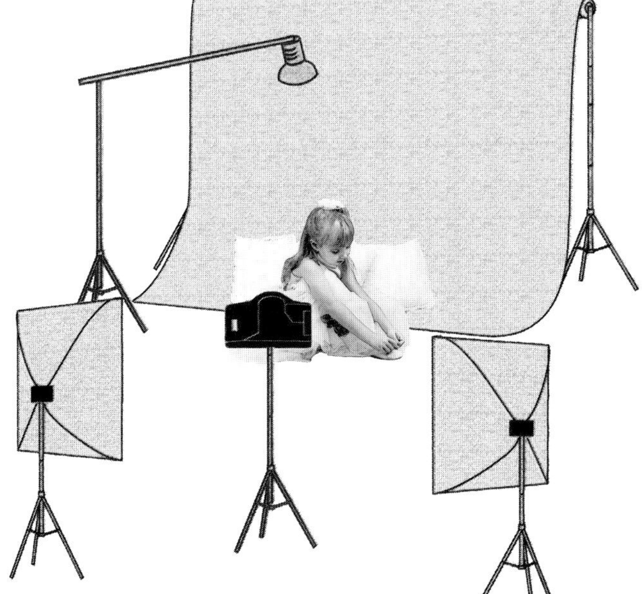

The main light for this shot comes from a softbox placed to the left of the camera. Another softbox is used at half-power from the right side of the camera to provide fill light. A hair light was added above the subject on a boom.

•Working with Schools

Our studio specializes in family and children's photography. A natural outcome of shooting a lot of kids is the work that we do with schools. We shoot quite a few dance schools, and they are actually a lot of fun. We usually shoot color but sometimes we have a chance to shoot black and white.

"We shoot quite a few dance schools ..."

•Recitals

Usually shoots happen in the Spring when the dance schools have their yearly performances. The dancers are dressed in their costumes and they come to the session with their makeup and hair done for the recital performance. It is wonderful to have each dancer perfectly made-up when they arrive.

•Bringing the Studio with Us

We use the normal studio lighting set-up,and move our whole studio to the location. We set up the lights just as we do in our permanent studio and use a portable background holder to set up various backdrops. We have several muslin backdrops that we use.The one in this photograph is our medium blue one. We adjust the value of the backdrop by varying the lighting on it. If we throw a lot of light on it, it goes very light. When we reduce the amount of light illuminating it, it can go very dark.

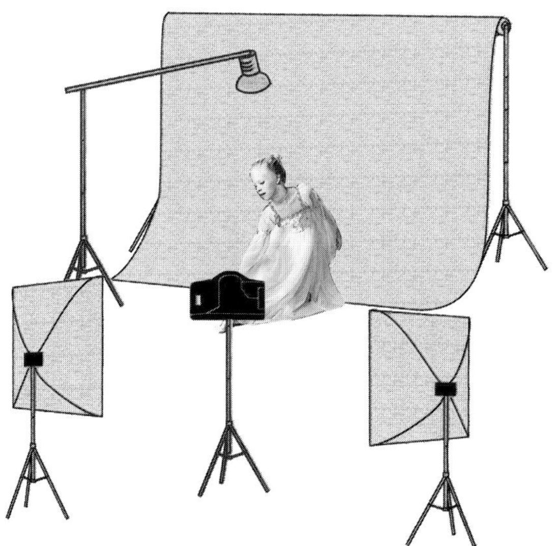

Camera: Canon EOS

Lens: 35-135mm zoom

Film: Kodak TMAX100 rated at E.I. 80

The main light for this shot comes from a softbox placed to the left of the camera. Another softbox is used at half-power from the right side of the camera to provide fill light. A hair light was added above the subject on a boom.

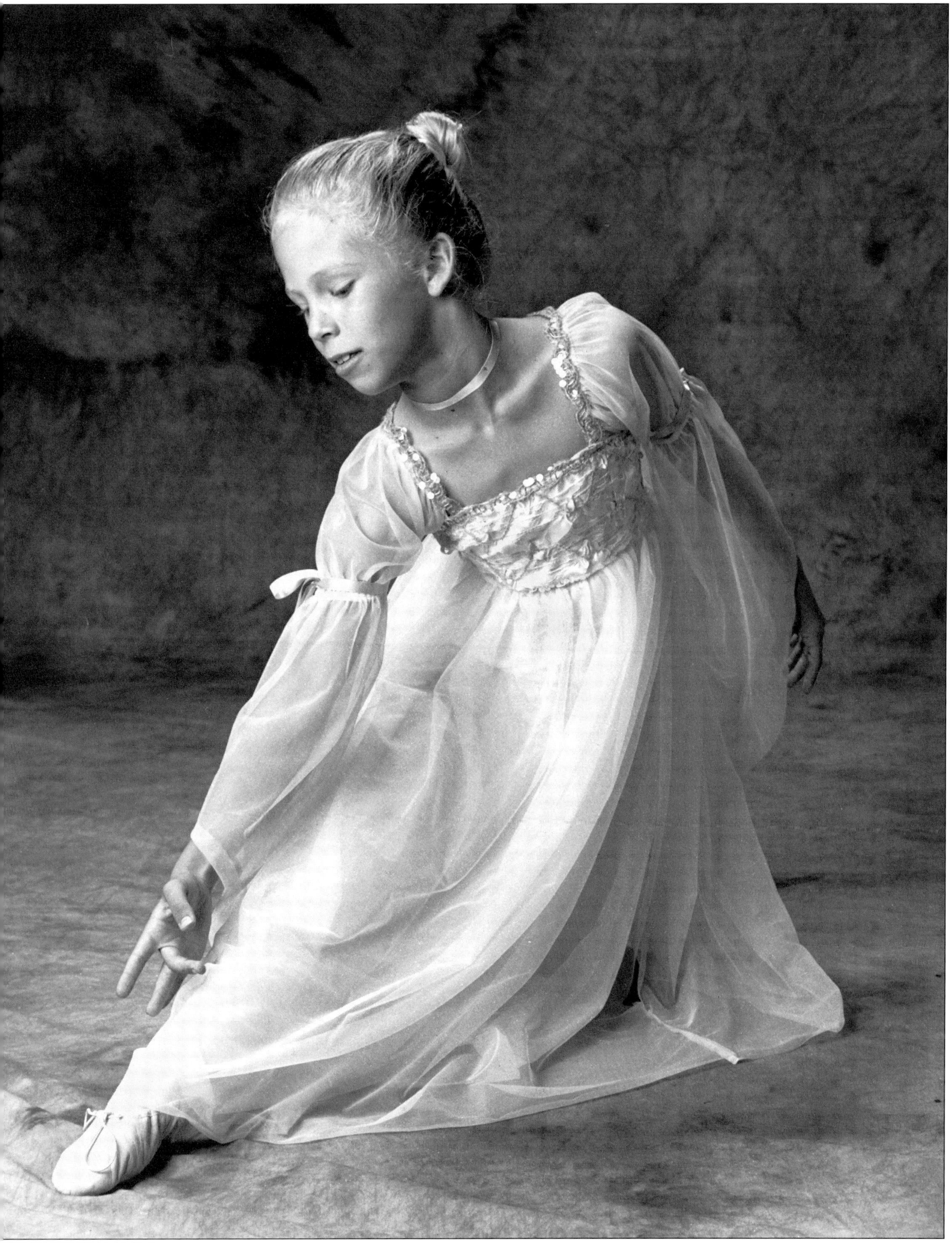

•Showing a Unique Personality

Just as bigger kids enjoy sports and dance, little ones love their toys. Adding a treasured toy to a portrait can put the child at ease and show his unique personality. This little boy wanted to bring along a very special toy, his small wooden horse.

"This little boy wanted to bring along a small wooden horse ..."

•Capturing Priceless Expressions

When two or three year olds are at the beach they just want to play in the sand and run away from the surf. During their play, ask them to show you their toy, or tell them a joke – get their attention so they will look up at you. This makes very natural shots that are true to the child's personality.

•Lighting

This boy was playing with his horse on the rocks with the sun setting directly behind him. We used a strong fill flash from the front to illuminate the deeper shadows and to keep the background well balanced with the foreground.

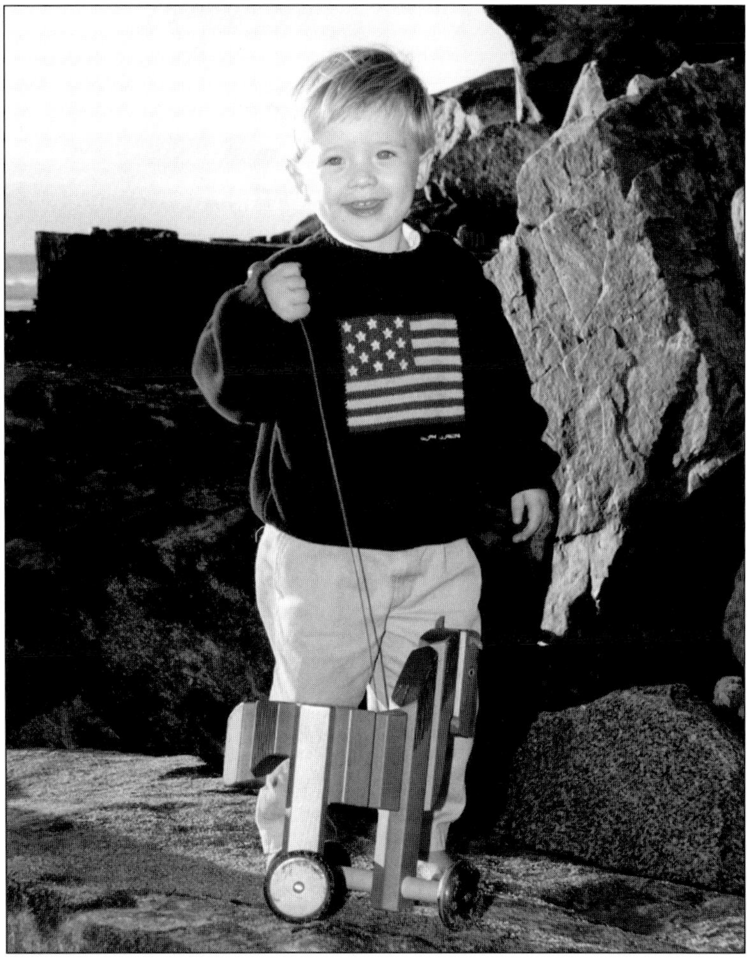

Camera: Canon EOS

Lens: 35-135mm zoom

Film: Kodak TMAX CN rated at E.I. 200

Adding Grown-ups

"The splendid thing about fathers and sons is that they can be so physical. The result can be portraits full of wonderful special energy."

•Getting Out of the Way

Sometimes, as a photographer, you just have to get out of the way. This is a very special and intimate moment between mother and child. It would be hard to capture such a moment if you were running around adjusting hair lights, setting the power on the background strobes, or trying to calculate your lighting ratios.

"Sometimes … you just have to get out of the way."

•Lighting

When you have a simple lighting set-up, you can concentrate on working with your clients and not worrying about technical lighting details. Often you don't need a lot of strobes and hair lights, just one main soft box and a reflector to kick back some light to open up the shadows.

The directional quality of the lighting in this portrait is required to show the texture in the clothing. And because this is such a soft feminine subject, it is important to keep the lighting soft by using a large diffuse light source.

•Background

We kept the background simple, just a dark background to give some contrast to the light clothing the subjects are wearing. This way you don't have to light the background at all. In fact just do the opposite; keep light off of it.

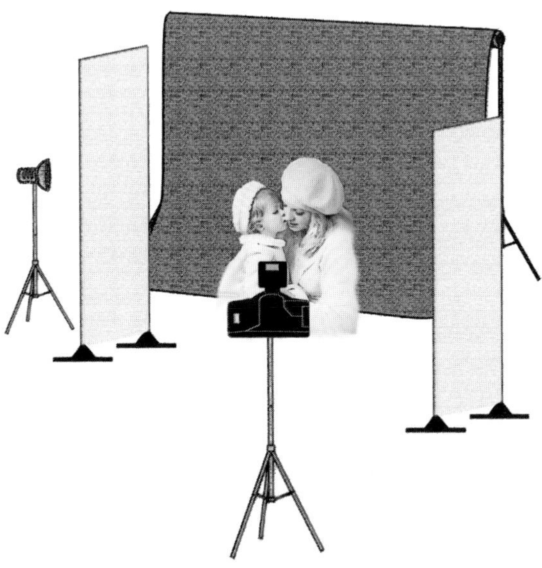

Camera: Canon RT

Lens: 35-135mm zoom

Film: Kodak TMAX CN 400, rated at E.I. 200

A tungsten light hits the background and subjects through a diffusion panel, and a reflector panel bounces some of this light back from the other side of the set. An on-camera flash completes the set-up.

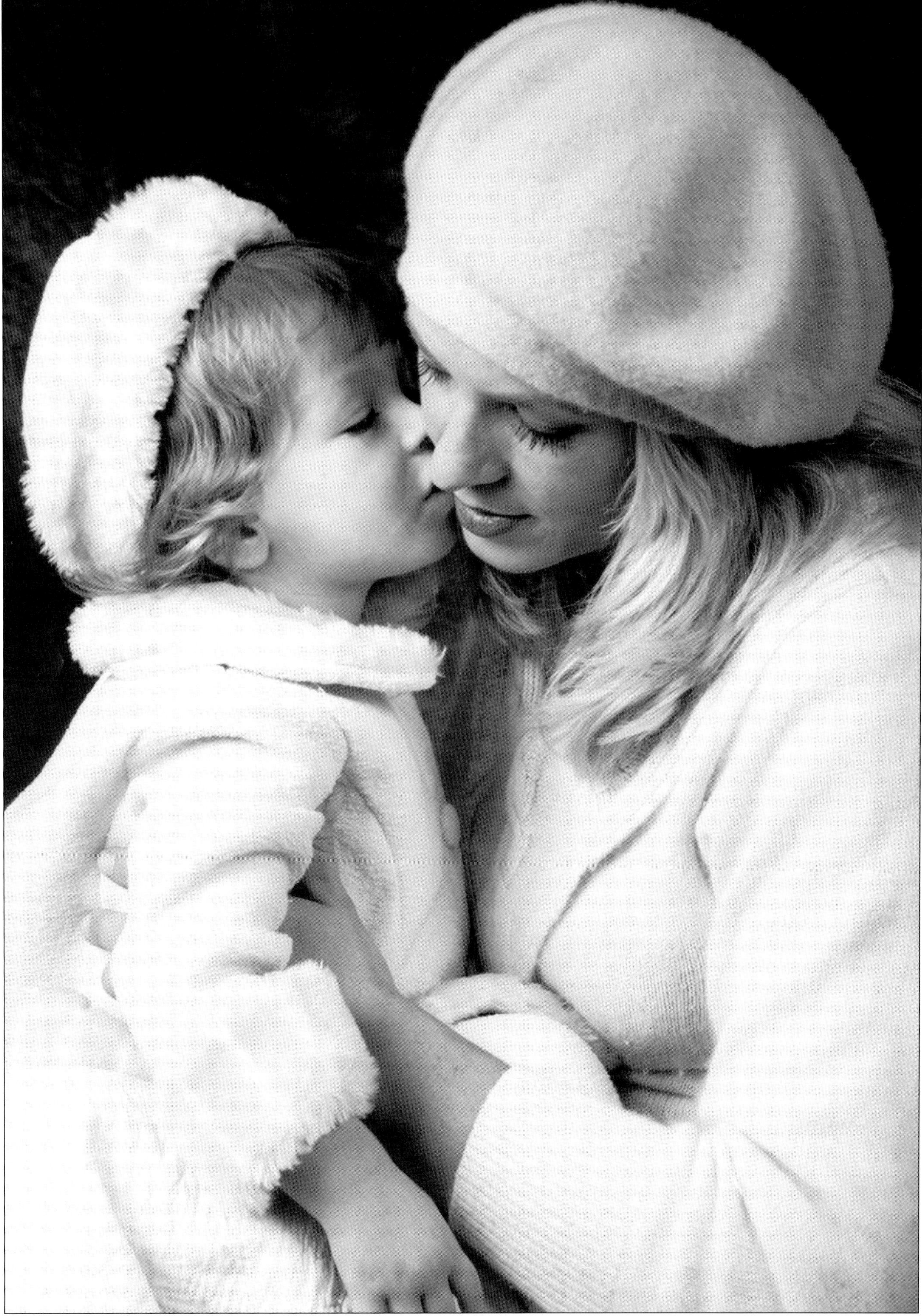

•Personality Types

Children are no different than the rest of us. They come in all types of temperaments; some are confident, some are reserved, some are self assured and some are shy.

This little girl was a little intimidated by the whole process of making a portrait. She was in a strange studio with unknown people pointing cameras at her – and all that's just fine. We don't try to "un-intimidate" a child. It just doesn't work, and more often than not it only makes matters worse. We try to deal with what we have – a clingy child. The best thing to do is try to work out a picture solution that will give the best results under the circumstances.

"This little girl was a little intimidated by the whole process ..."

•An Informal Portrait

This informal portrait is enhanced by the mom reaching down and giving some comfort and security to her daughter. It's natural for children to hold onto their mother and find solace in being close to her. Just the manner in which the little girl's tiny foot is positioned on top of her mom's foot speaks volumes about their relationship. The statement of scale is also important to this portrait. You can tell the age of the child by her height compared to the mom's height.

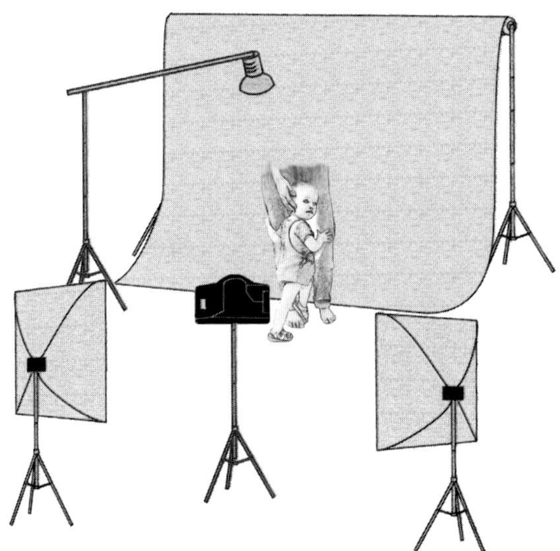

Camera: Canon EOS 630

Lens: 50mm

Film: Ilford XP1, rated at E.I. 200

The main light for this shot comes from a softbox placed to the left of the camera. Another softbox is used at half-power from the right side of the camera to provide fill light. A hair light was added above the subject on a boom.

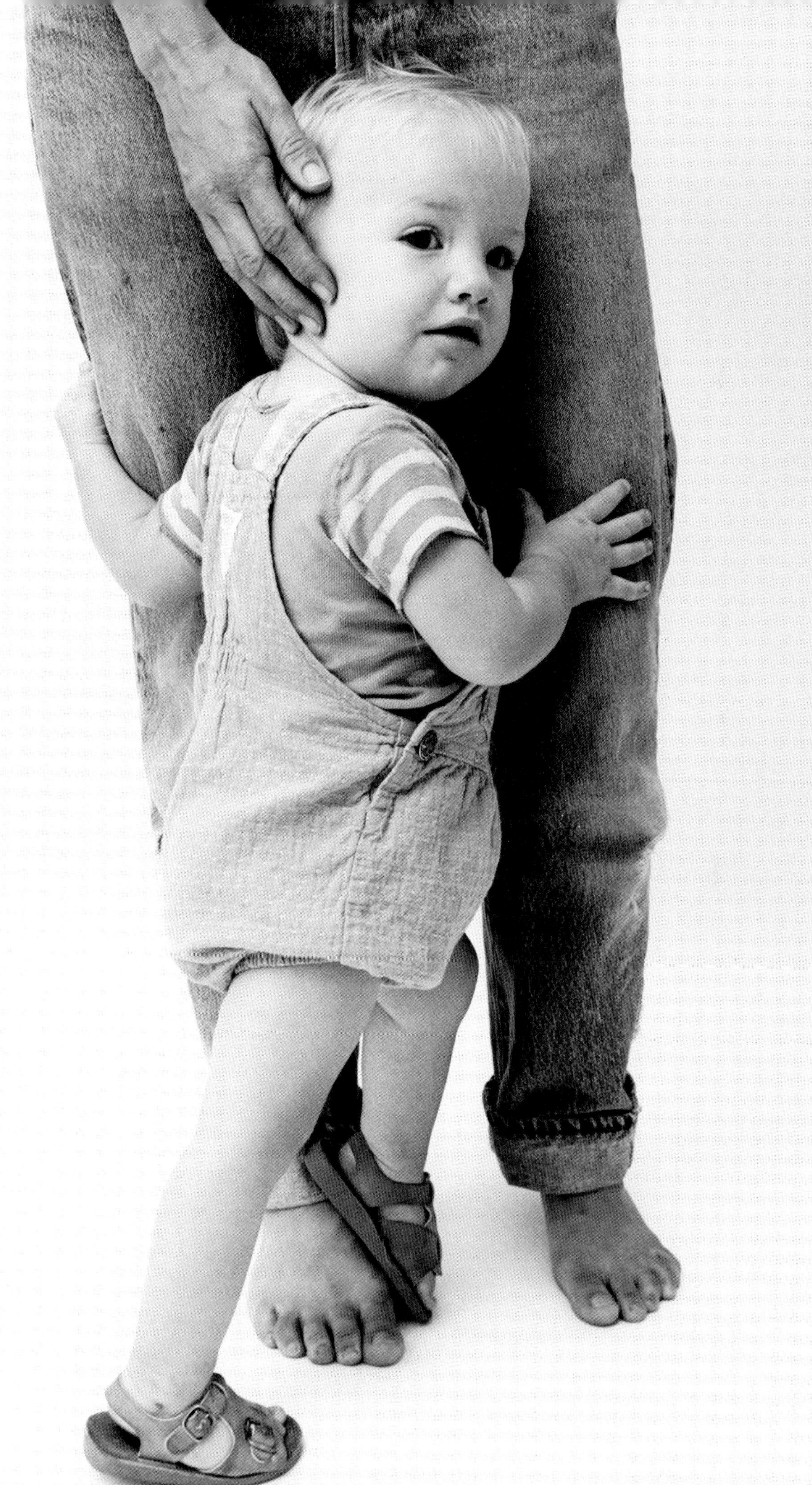

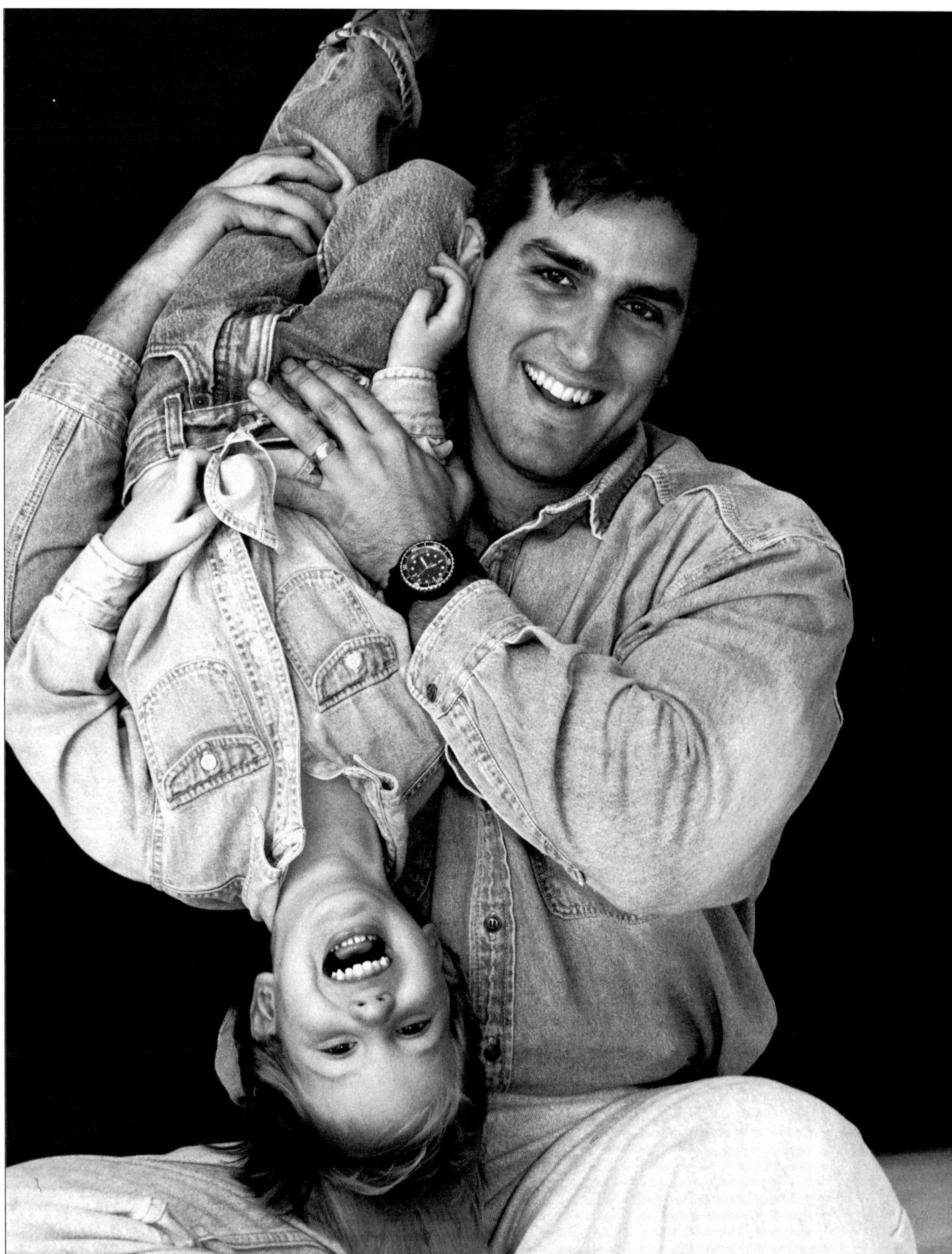

"... they really know how to play with their kids."

•High Energy

This is one of our favorite father and son photos. It is great to have dads in the studio – they really know how to play with their kids. They can wrestle and throw them around and the kids just eat it up. We try our best to loosen up the dads and the kids to get them to relax and play. The splendid thing about fathers and sons is that they can be so physical. The result can be portraits full of wonderful special energy.

•Lighting

When we first started out we tried out many different lighting systems until we settled on the system that we use now; large soft boxes with power packs and strobes. An earlier system used an on-camera flash. It triggered a strobe light by using either a slave plugged into the power pack or an infrared triggering system. We put a diffuser on the on-camera flash to soften the light, or sometimes we would bounce the light off the ceiling to diffuse it even more. In this shot, we placed the main strobe light behind a five foot tall translucent nylon panel that acted just like a large soft box.

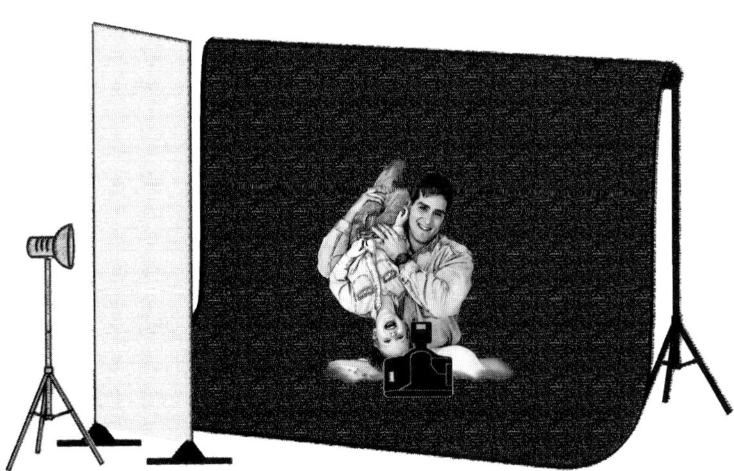

Camera: Canon EOS 630

Lens: 35-135mm zoom

Film: Ilford XP1, rated at E.I. 200

The main strobe light was placed behind a large (five foot tall) nylon panel – making it act just like a large soft box. An on-camera flash triggered the main strobe. The on-camera flash can be either bounced off the ceiling or fitted with a diffuser to soften it.

•Posing

You really have to work to get good original maternity pictures. We always think it's special to include the siblings in these pictures. We enjoy the idea of smaller children relating to their baby brother or sister while he or she is in mom's tummy. The children can lay their hand on the tummy to try to feel the baby moving. Sometimes they press their ear against the mother's stomach to see if they can hear the baby's heartbeat. You can even try to coax them into giving the new baby a kiss.

"Sometimes they press their ear against the mother's stomach ..."

It's hard to get a child, the mom's face, and her tummy all together in the same shot. So we have to crop the top of the mom. There is no need to show her face; it's evident who she is.

•Mom's Clothing

Frequently we drape the mom's stomach in some fashion. Here the her hand is holding the gown to show the shape of her abdomen.

•Backdrop

For the background we used a sheer drape. We used clips to form folds in the background. This is preferable to a plain solid background and it adds some interest without taking attention away from the main subject matter.

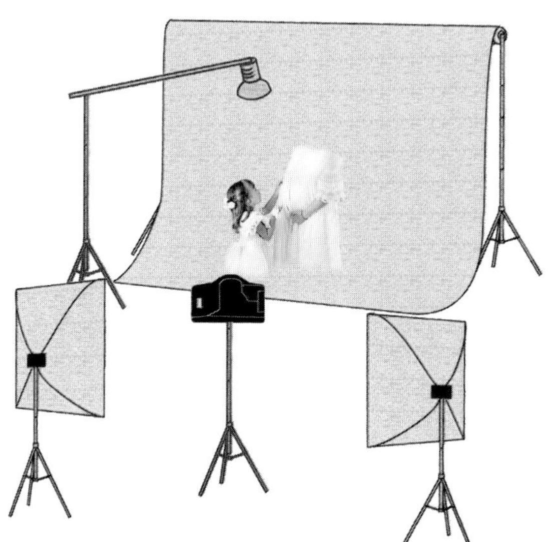

Camera: Pentax 645 on a tripod
Lens: 75mm leaf shutter
Film: Kodak TMX100

The main light for this shot comes from a softbox placed to the left of the camera. Another softbox is used at half-power from the right side of the camera to provide fill light. A hair light was added above the subjects on a boom.

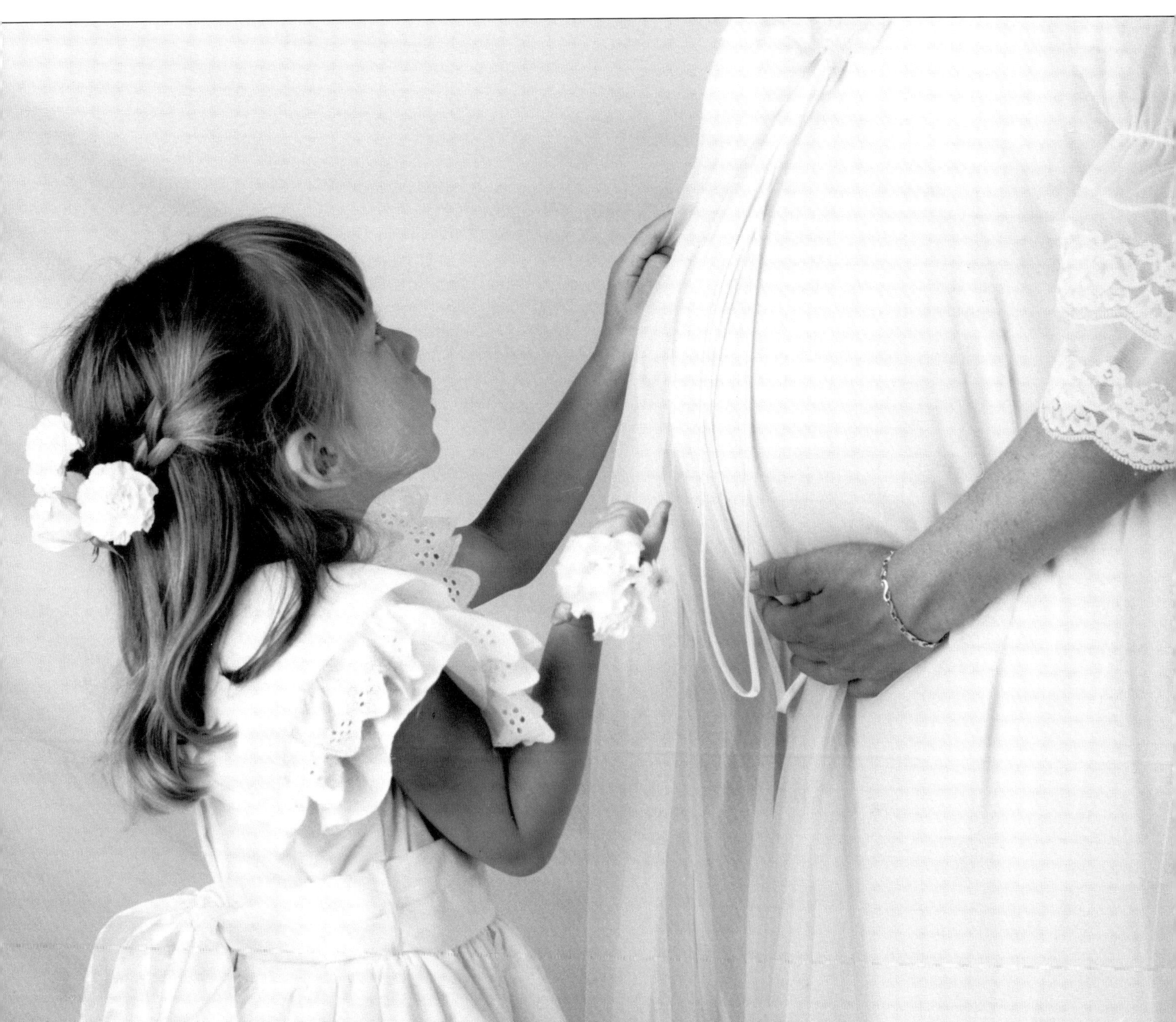

•Family History

This picture portrays a great-grandmother and her two baby great-grand-daughters. It's so important for the children to have this picture as an heirloom or keepsake. With today's increased interest in genealogy, portraits like these are also valuable as a reference to family history.

"... portraits ... are also valuable as a reference to family history."

•Doing it for the Kids

Much of the time, older people do not want to get their picture taken. Some senior citizens are not comfortable with the way they look. Still, we always try to get them into the the portrait session so that the younger family members have pictures of themselves with their grandparents or great-grandparents. Emphasize that this is not something you're doing for the adult, but that it's something you want to do for the children.

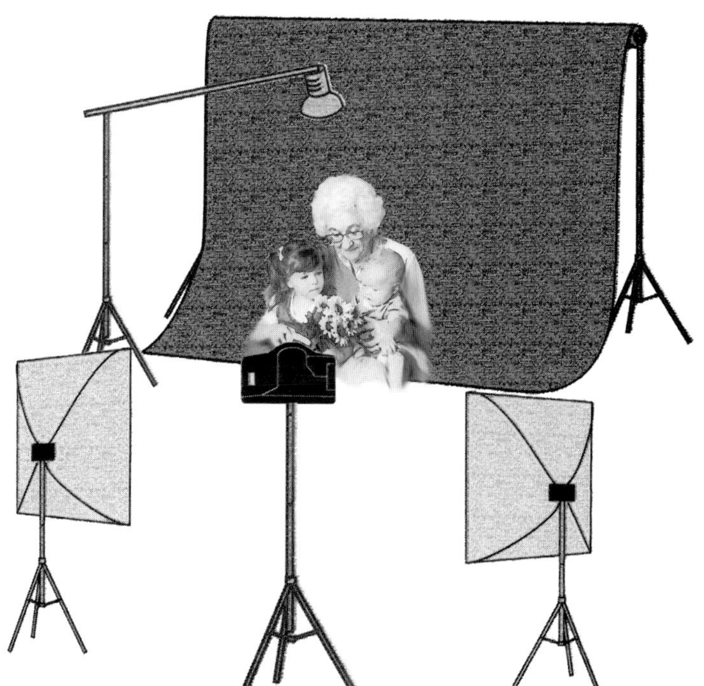

Camera: Canon EOS RT

Lens: 35-135mm zoom

Film: Ilford XP2, rated at E.I. 200

The main light for this shot comes from a softbox placed to the left of the camera. Another softbox is used at half-power from the right side of the camera to provide fill light. A hair light was added above the subjects on a boom. A darker backdrop was used to emphasize the grandmother's white hair.

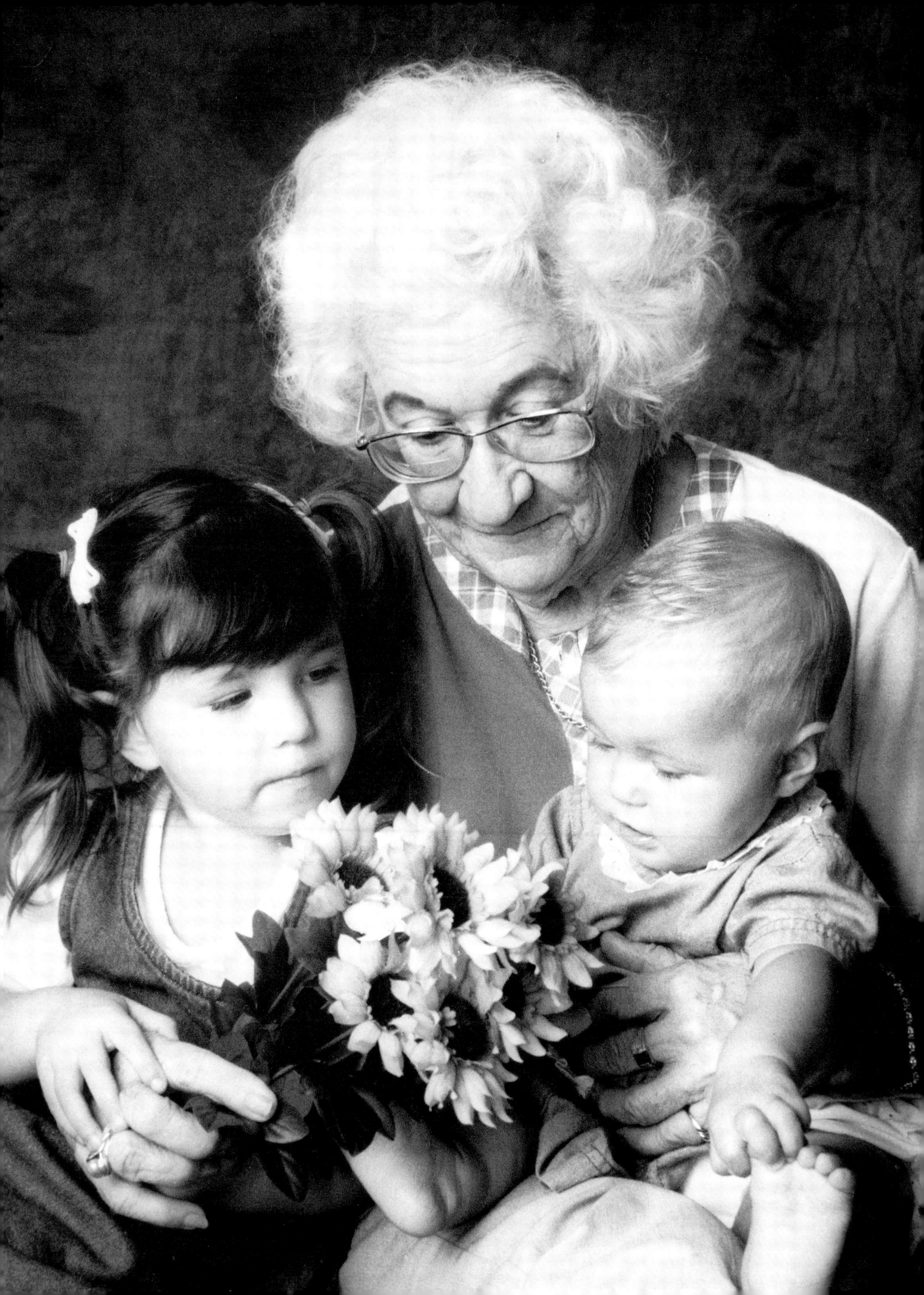

•Importance of Getting Dad in the Picture

It's wonderful when I get fathers in the studio to have portraits taken with their babies. Buying a portrait session for the family is something that isn't even on the radar screen for most men. They sometimes are very busy and schedules are so hectic that it's difficult for them to make it to the studio appointments with their families. We feel very strongly that it is important to have these one-on-one pictures to give to their children and themselves.

•Posing

These two don't seem to be posing for the camera. They are having a personal father/child moment, and the photographer is there just as an observer to record the moment – not as an active participant. This is a classic pose reminiscent of a madonna and child artistic composition. We've just used the characteristic pose with a father and child.

"These two don't seem to be posing for the camera."

•Composition

We've also cropped much of the father's image and made sure that all of the baby is included in the picture. This, along with the darkness of the father's clothing contrasted with the light skin tones of the baby, focuses all of our attention on the baby.

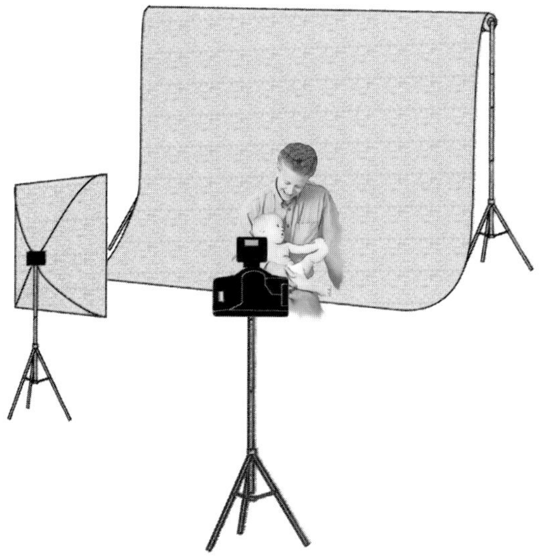

Camera: Canon EOS 630

Lens: 50mm

Film: Ilford XP1, rated at E.I. 200

A soft box to the left of the camera provided the main light for this portrait. The on-camera flash was bounced off the ceiling above the subjects to provide fill and accent lighting.

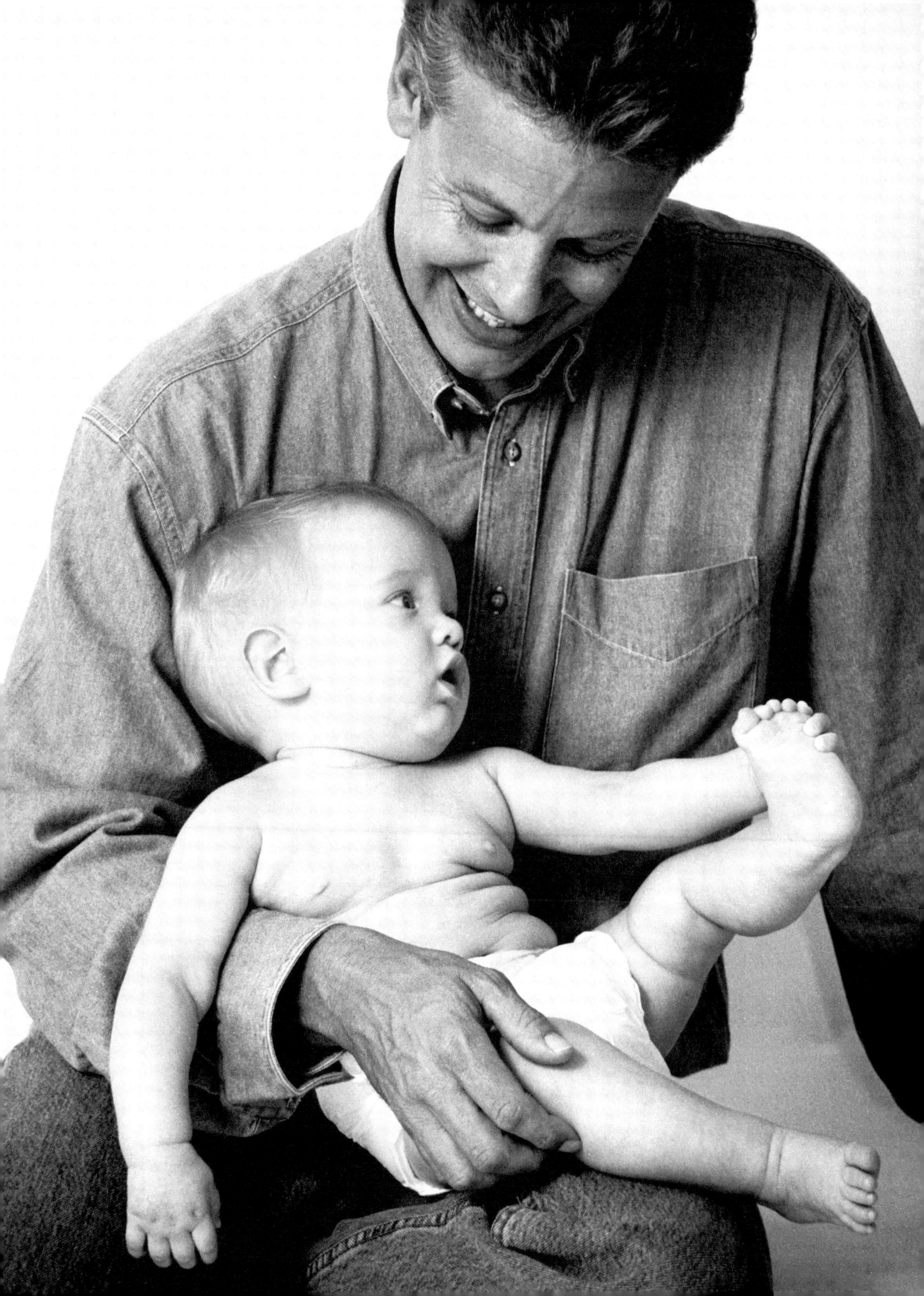

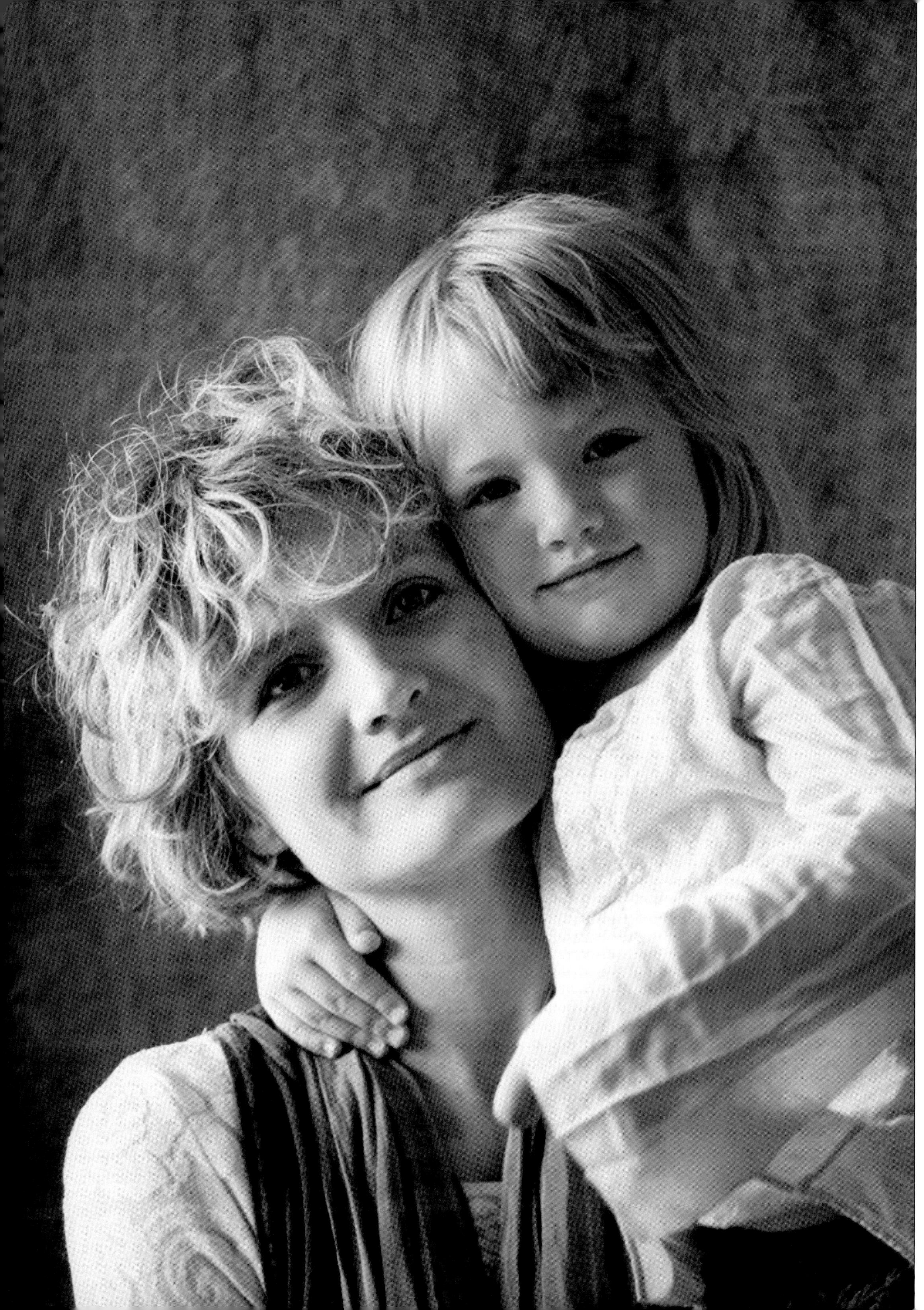

"... you get a sense of the physical and emotional closeness ..."

•Serenity

There is such a feeling of serenity in this portrait. It reveals how comfortable the mom and daughter are with each other. Their expressions are very relaxed and peaceful. By having the two press their cheeks together you get a sense of the physical and emotional closeness of the pair. It also shows how similar the mother and daughter look.

•Posing

For this shot, the mom sat down and her daughter stood in her lap. What really makes this photo different is the fact that the child is placed higher that the parent. It's not something that one is really even aware of, but you know there's a little something different in this photo. It's a lot of fun to mix up the rules sometimes when it comes to posing or composition. It makes the portraits a little unusual and gives the clients the sense that their portraits are unique.

•Lighting

This photo was lit by window light on the left side of the photograph and a reflector placed just out of the frame on the right. The reflector panel kicks back some light to fill in the shadows on the subjects' faces.

Camera: Canon EOS 630

Lens: 50mm

Film: Ilford XP1, rated at E.I. 200

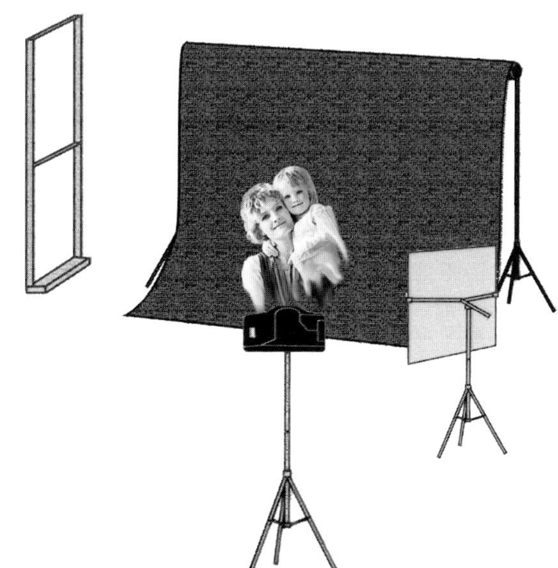

Window light from the left side of the camera is the main light for this portrait. Fill light is provided by a reflector placed just out of frame to the right of the camera.

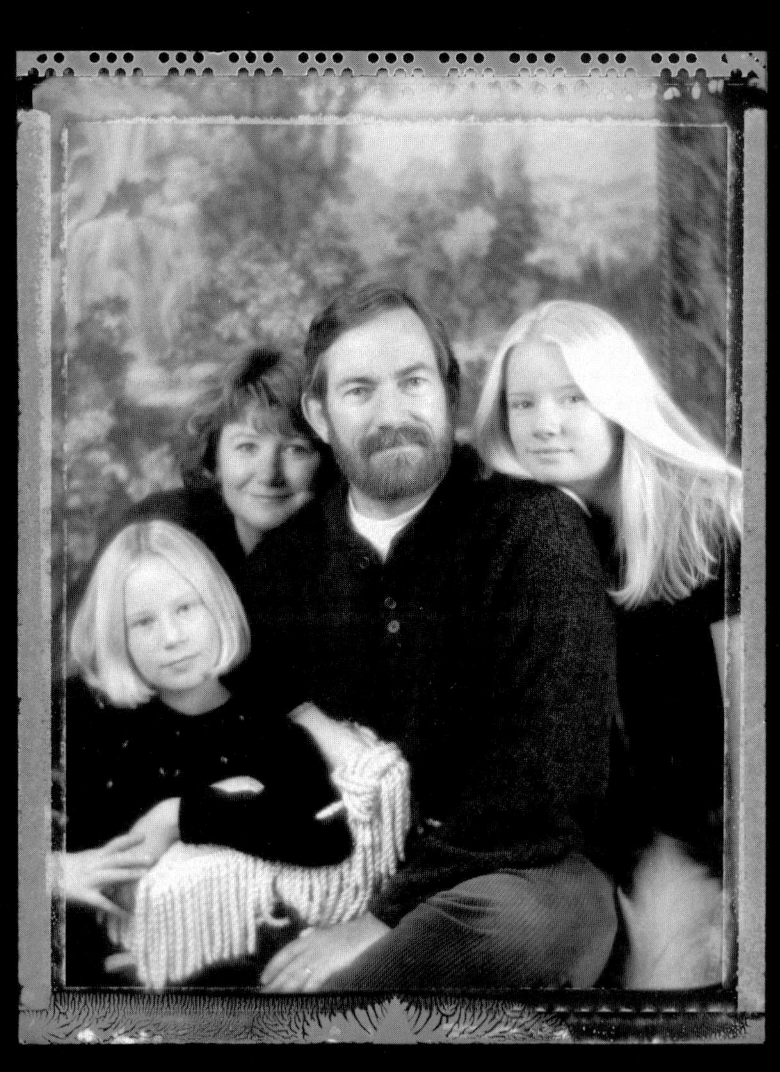

"It is so difficult to get a good photograph of photographers."

•Photographing The Photographer

It is so difficult to get a good photograph of photographers. Every photographer should go through the experience of taking their own portrait in their own studio so they can better empathize with their clients – from getting ready for the session all the way through to print selection.

•Make it a Family Project

This is a family self-portrait that we produced as a family project. We worked with a 4x5 camera, Polaroid type 55 P/N film, and a long air bulb shutter release. The Polaroid film allowed us to preview our posing, lighting and facial expressions and produced a 4x5 black and white negative that we used to make prints.

•Posing

Ian, my husband, is "grounded" in the center, and my girls Sara and Chelsea are placed on either side. I am in the back with the shutter release to expose the film after setting up the lighting, posing and camera settings. We used a large wall tapestry hung on a movable stand for the backdrop. It gives the photograph a "renaissance" feeling to it.

Camera: 4x5 Linhof Master Technika
Lens: 250mm portrait lens
Film: Polaroid Type 55 Positive/Negative

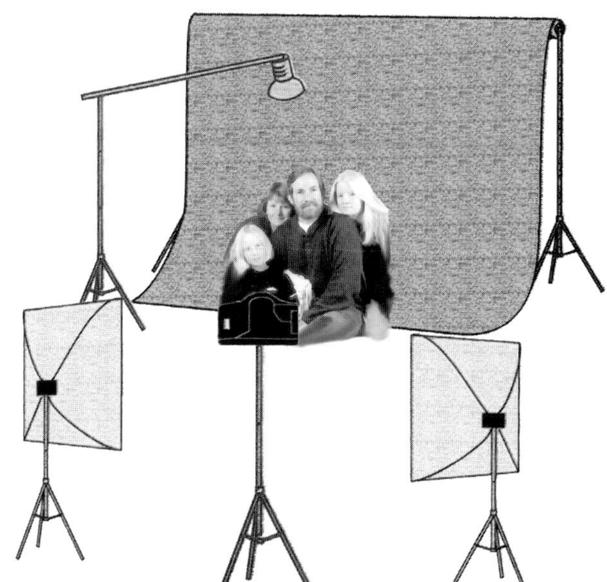

The main light for this shot comes from a softbox placed to the left of the camera. Another softbox is used at half-power from the right side of the camera to provide fill light.

•Hand Tinting and Archival Quality

While I was in college I was introduced to the art of hand tinting black and white photos. This would become one of the most important things that I learned in school that would help me with my black and white photography. I taught art classes and held hand tinting workshops for a while before our studio became too busy. I have always liked to teach and share with other people what I have learned.

I have always felt very strongly about the permanence of black and white photography. If the photographs are processed in an archival manner on fiber based papers, toned, and displayed properly, they should last for generations. These are truly heirlooms that you are creating. When you add the hand tint with oil colors, you are recreating the old way of producing color photography.

"These are truly heirlooms that you are creating."

When I hand over portraits that have so much integrity, I feel proud that I have created them and I know that they are the best I can give to my customers.

If you have never tried black and white film, or haven't tried it in many years, give it a try and have some more fun.

Other Books from Amherst Media, Inc.

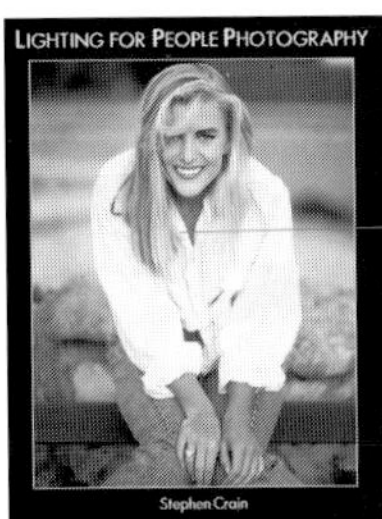

Lighting for People Photography

Stephen Crain

The complete guide to lighting. Includes: set-ups, equipment information, how to control strobe and natural lighting, and much more! Features diagrams, illustrations, and exercises for practicing the lighting techniques discussed in each chapter. $29.95 list, 8½x11, 112p, b&w and color photos, glossary, index, order no. 1296.

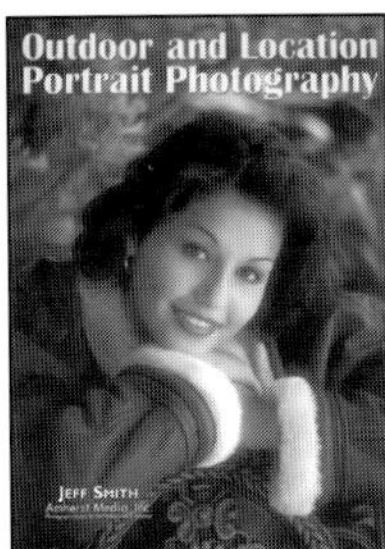

Outdoor and Location Portrait Photography

Jeff Smith

Learn how to work with natural light, select the best locations, and make clients look their best. Step-by-step discussions and helpful illustrations teach you the techniques you need to shoot outdoor portraits like a pro! $29.95 list, 8½x11, 128p, b&w and color photos, index, order no. 1632.

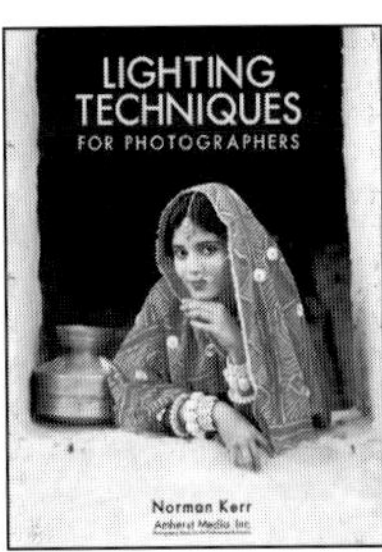

Lighting Techniques for Photographers

Norm Kerr

This book teaches you to predict the effects of light in the final image. It covers the interplay of light qualities, as well as color compensation and manipulation of light and shadow. $29.95 list, 8½x11, 120p, 150+ color and b&w photos, index, order no. 1564.

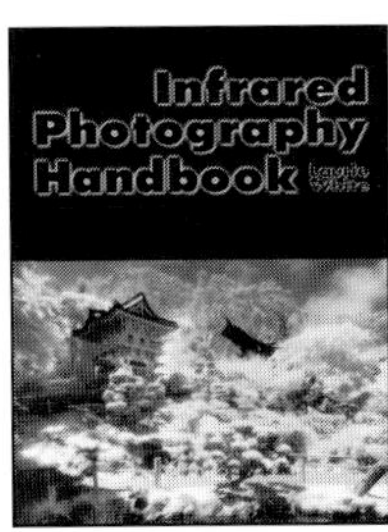

Infrared Photography Handbook

Laurie White

Covers black and white infrared photography: focus, lenses, film loading, film speed rating, batch testing, paper stocks, and filters. Black & white photos illustrate how IR film reacts. $24.95 list, 8½x11, 104p, 50 b&w photos, charts & diagrams, order no. 1419.

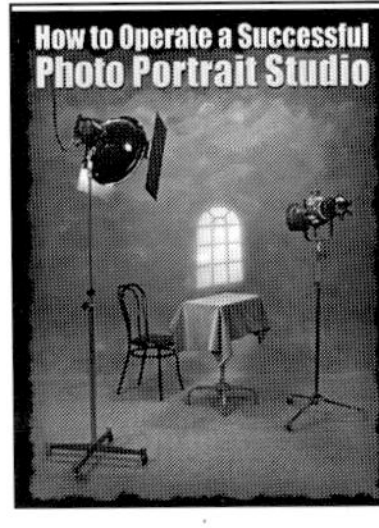

How to Operate a Successful Photo Portrait Studio

John Giolas

Combines photographic techniques with practical business information to create a complete guide book for anyone interested in developing a portrait photography business. $29.95 list, 8½x11, 120p, 120 photos, index, order no. 1579.

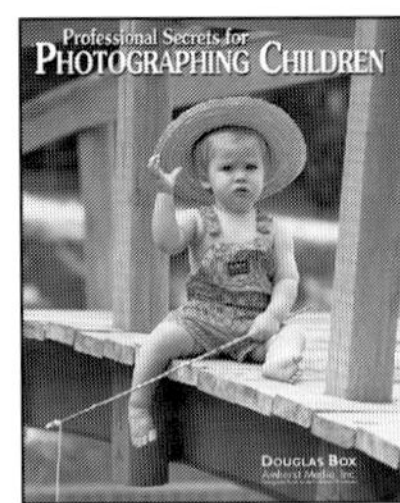

Professional Secrets for Photographing Children

Douglas Allen Box

Covers every aspect of photographing children on location and in the studio. Prepare children and parents for the shoot, capture a child's personality, and shoot story book themes. $29.95 list, 8½x11, 128p, 74 photos, index, order no. 1635.

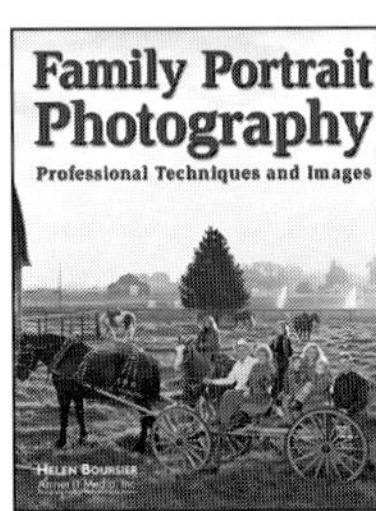

Family Portrait Photography

Helen Boursier

Tells how to operate a successful portrait studio, including marketing family portraits, advertising, working with clients, posing, lighting, and selection of equipment. $29.95 list, 8½x11, 120p, 123 photos, index, order no. 1629.

More Photo Books Are Available!

Write or fax for a *FREE* catalog:

AMHERST MEDIA, INC.
PO BOX 586
AMHERST, NY 14226 USA

Fax: 716-874-4508

Ordering & Sales Information:

INDIVIDUALS: If possible, purchase books from an Amherst Media retailer. Write to us for the dealer nearest you. To order direct, send a check or money order with a note listing the books you want and your shipping address. U.S. & overseas freight charges are $3.50 first book and $1.00 for each additional book. Visa and Master Card accepted. New York state residents add 8% sales tax.

DEALERS, DISTRIBUTORS & COLLEGES: Write, call or fax to place orders. For price information, contact Amherst Media or an Amherst Media sales representative. Net 30 days.

All prices, publication dates, and specifications are subject to change without notice.

Prices are in U.S. dollars. Payment in U.S. funds only.